Facebreak

The Hidden Side of How Texting, Liking, and Stalking Impact Our Relationships

If you would like to keep updated on the release of future books, my blog posts, and speaking engagements please click on the link below to subscribe to my newsletter.

Dave's Newsletter

I respect your privacy and will never share your email address or personal information.

Chapter One

The Purpose of This Book

I consult and counsel business professionals for a living. I work directly with my clients one-on-one, and in almost all cases I help them with their marriage or relationships.

Although businesses have their own specific problems related specifically to management, selling and marketing, etc, many of the problems professionals have are not rooted in their businesses themselves, but rather the *communication problems* that arise within their own marriages or relationships.

In fact much of the so called "stress" that people talk about comes from conversations they've had that were upsetting or taken out of context be it with their partner or spouse or even online.

Enter Facebook.

I'm not here to bash Facebook. Facebook has its merits. With Facebook I get to keep up with my family and friends when in truth that was only done previously by email or phone. And rarely then because who calls their brother or sister that often *just* to hear about their daughter's soccer game?

Exactly.

But I am here to talk about the side of Facebook that, interestingly enough, people shy away from. That murky ground of things said or done online which were seemingly harmless actions but ended in upset.

You can get lots of likes or views, *loves*, even, on a sunrise picture or cute puppy video, but when you ask people to open up about the their experiences with Instant Messaging or Scrolling on Facebook, *whoooweee!* People do not want to go there!

Well, enough people answered my surveys so with this book, *I am going there.* And for a reason.

Facebook is like the Wild Wild West. It's unchartered ground in terms of the rules. Are there any rules? In truth there really aren't unless you're talking about a specific Facebook *group.* And then the rules are written there, enforced by faceless moderators. But your own or another's personal Newsfeed? That's just Dodge City with no Sheriff. That's you on the playground at school with no teacher or Student Assistant patrolling.

And I'm sure there's a little bit in all of us that likes the fact that there are no teachers on the school ground. There's some kind of teenage James Dean DNA coursing through all our collective veins. You know, *"Can I ditch my Geometry class and get away with it?"* It's that basic mischievous impulse that is most likely inherent in all of us. And there's nothing wrong with good healthy mischief.

But when the mischief crosses a line, *then we have a problem.*

The purpose of this book is to bring a better understanding of where that line is, how it gets crossed, (wittingly or unwittingly) the ramifications, and some insight in how to stay above it.

I am not here to offer any hard line rules or some dogma one should follow. Even in the Wild West if you had a beef there was at least an agreed upon (yet unspoken) code to settle it outside the saloon. You knew you'd have to stand a certain distance apart and hope you were the fastest draw. You don't even have that on Facebook. There's no saloon or a shot of whiskey you can take a swig of. In fact you don't even feel the bullet until later when you find out you were unfriended while you were asleep!

By offering some advice and insight here, my purpose is to show you how you can at least keep your own "antenna" up to avoid any potential harm or upset to yourself or others.

I named this book "Facebreak" because in truth the answers to my surveys showed that there were numerous examples of great communications occurring between you and a friend, spouse, or colleague that then went off the rails *via* Facebook.

There was in fact a *break* in communication, causing what I call a *FaceBreak*.

After working with individuals and couples for over forty years, I hope this book offers you some insight whereby you can avoid the *Facebreaks*, and enjoy the tremendous upsides Facebook provides to increase your communication and stay in touch with those you love, admire, and respect.

Dave Worthen

Chapter Two

The Invisible Line

There is a line. But is it *invisible?*

No, not really.

We've all screwed up and done something unethical. Like when you were a kid and you stole that piece of bubblegum from the hundreds that were in the store bin. You *crossed a line.*

Even if you got away with it, you *still* crossed the line. In fact the moment your hand grabbed that piece of gum and you didn't pay for it, you knew inherently that that line had been crossed.

That is an *ethical* line. Don't worry. I'm not going to get all pulpit-preachy here. You can call it ethics or integrity or whatever you like. It's an inherent part of *who you are.* When you tape a tiny piece of paper under your shirt sleeve as a cheat sheet just before a test, you know what you are doing. You are cheating. There's no rule book you can go to on page fifteen that tells you this. You just *know* it.

When you're in a relationship with someone you love and you click on the picture of someone of the opposite sex *it can seem innocuous.*

And it may very well be.

But if it even slightly *"pings"* inside you---and I mean even for *one-billionth of a second* you had the thought "I probably shouldn't" or "I wonder if Jennifer/Greg would mind?" *Anything* that makes you *take pause,* you have just come "face to face" with this invisible line.

The truth is that line is in each of us. And when you cross it, you cross it uniquely as you. You can (and people do) get into moral debates about what is cheating or crossing the line. There's no need for debate. You're not voting for a Senator.

THIS IS YOUR OWN PERSONAL RELATIONSHIP WITH THIS INVISIBLE LINE.

And if you are alone, there are most likely no ramifications other than your own *knowledge* that you might have crossed a line, "but no big deal." "No harm no foul."

But when you have a partner or spouse, then you're going to have to be on the same page. Because if your wife is ogling men with abs that you don't have, or you are ogling women with boobs she doesn't have, and this is not known between you, well it doesn't take me telling you here in this sentence that you're going to have a problem.

If you don't think so, then just invite your partner or spouse to sit down with you as you click away and see if you click the same things you'd click alone.

Here's the thing: When you log onto Facebook, you are basically in a virtual world. There's no Sheriff. There's no Marshall Dillon to greet you in Dodge City and go over the rules. Facebook has their own protection for legal recourse, but really if you want to flirt with a girl or guy while you're both "facebooking" while sitting on the couch together, there is nothing to stop you. And even if you are not flirting---because this is where that invisible line comes in---*you are involving yourself in conduct that may boomerang on you.*

Here's an example out in real life: You have probably experienced sometime in your life driving alone out on a country road in the middle of nowhere or in remote city at 2:00 a.m. and you come upon a red light. There's not a soul anywhere. Just you and the red light.

You *stop*, because hello---*you stop at red lights.* And then you get impatient because out in the middle of nowhere or at 2:00 a.m. you just don't want to wait for it to turn green. So you go ahead and run it. And your life goes on. Sure, you look back through your rearview mirror because why? Because innately you know you just ran a red light and you wanted to make sure no black and white units were going to pull out from wherever they were hiding to now bust you.

Yet this is not about red lights, stopping, or cops.

This is simply your decision to act in a way that may (or may not) have repercussions. And to take this example out to its extreme, let's say a week later you get an official looking envelope in the mail and you open it up. It's got a grainy picture of your car and license plate running the red light at 2:03 a.m. with a fine of $157.00.

You're *incredulous*, right?

Well, that's about the way some of the answers on the survey came out. Wives and husbands and partners *incredulous* at the fact of *who and what was clicked on.* Surprise. Disappointment. Even jealousy.

Did I say *boomerang?*

Integrity & The Invisible Line:

Let's take a look at this idea of integrity because it plays a huge role in this Facebook experience.

The concept of integrity originally comes from a Middle English derivation that basically means *wholeness, completeness,* or being *untouched.* Visualize in your mind a simple white circle. That is *your integrity.* Then you "Like" or Comment or *do something* that you possibly felt an *ever-so-slight twinge of guilt.* After you did this, the feeling stuck around.

And now this act puts this *teeny-tiny*, almost *microscopic dot* on that white circle. Your integrity to that degree *is less whole.*

And the ironic thing is that teeny-tiny microscopic dot in truth now becomes this *black hole where your attention gets stuck.* You *know* this.

Then, your wife or husband, while they're scrolling Facebook, notice that you have liked a guy or girl that is *also* a friend of theirs. And what makes this murky is often these "friends" are not necessarily real world friends each of you *really know.* Or possibly you do know them and they're recently single or divorced or have a "reputation" of some sort.

Well let's just freeze frame this right here.

Your wife comes over to you and she shows you her iPad. It's open to Facebook and she asks, *"So...how do you know Cindy?"*

Gulp.

See?

If there was no invisible line crossed there is no *Gulp.* It gets sorted out with a rational answer. *"She's a Project Manager for one of your clients and you were just "Liking" it as part of your relationship."*

Your wife is *good.* You're *good.*

But there is still this *moment* that has been largely ignored by most people going through these experiences on Facebook.

And that is that moment when you *do* interact in the virtual world you are going to have to take a tad more responsibility for your actions. Just like *"nobody around at the red light."* That's not a *completely* responsible viewpoint. Which is why it can *boomerang.*

So when you click on "Like" or you run the red light it's all going to be your chess move that *you have to own.* You cannot then complain about the ticket. You cannot then get irate with your spouse for asking. There is no such thing as an action of any kind that you are not in part or wholly responsible for.

Telling the Truth:

The next question becomes have you told your wife or husband the truth?

If you are the wife, are you sure "*all is good*" or do you have some microscopic attention still on your husband clicking on Cindy's picture? Maybe his explanation was totally legit. But does he fantasize about Cindy? She's *awfully attractive*, you think to yourself.

Examine for yourself when *you yourself* have experienced this flow.

You found your partner had liked someone a tad bit more than it was easy for you to experience. And it doesn't matter *why*.

It matters that it did.

One could chime in that this whole idea of interaction in the virtual world should just be carefree. Some will say that trying to put some kind of ethics or integrity in will be too restrictive. This is Facebook after all where you can see cat videos and waterfalls in New Zealand.

Well, here's the truth: The red light in the middle of nowhere at 2:00 a.m. is a red light in the middle of nowhere at 2:00 a.m. Restriction has *nothing* to do with the red light.

You assign the restriction to the red light.

Listen. If you're "not-really-flirting" on Facebook with a guy you're chummy with at work, then there's a simple handling: Just invite your boyfriend to sit in with you as you do your thing with your co-worker online. You know, like you're both watching a Netflix movie.

See what I mean about the invisible line?

Where The Hell is This Line?

Of course the line is there. It's just *inside you.* People have upsets because of what happens on the physical site of Facebook. Well, when the little kid first decided to steal the bubblegum, looked around to make sure no one saw him, he was already contemplating crossing that line. *But the line was inside him.* When he stuck his hand in the bin that is where the transgression occurred. And the word *transgression* is not biblical. It's actually Latin. It means to *step across.*

The real question is: Where was the step across *born?* That's right. In the beings *decision to do it.* He wouldn't have had to "make sure the coast is clear" if there was no "step across." Before you clicked on "Like" you either were clean with it or you decided to cross that line.

Once the action is done, then comes the other part: Justifying *why* you did it. See that's where the communication wars start. Couples are going back and forth about how it bothered one or the other that pictures were being "Liked" in a rather secretive fashion. These actions spawned jealousy. The jealousy spawned further *Facebreaks.*

But let's back this video up. What if you and your partner had made an agreement as to what is "stepping across?" Or what the line is?

That in fact makes the difference between having no attention on the actions you're involved in and scrolling and Liking away, and being somewhat if not totally secretive. Which when you involve yourself in those secretive kinds of actions your integrity takes a hit and you are in essence splintering your relationship with a keystroke.

The invisible line is etched in *your* soul. It is a line drawn from the very essence of *who you are.* Your mind knows where the line is. It's *your* mind. You cannot kid yourself when you cross it. And you certainly cannot kid your partner because they are part of that line.

Chapter Three

Are You Texting Me While I'm Texting You?

Probably one of the highest survey question answers that was aggravating for both parties in a relationship was when one person was texting their partner (or colleague) and the other person was doing the same. The little "three dot bubble" that hovers just over the text space makes this cute little sound when the other person is texting or replying back.

But it is not so cute when you are texting or replying back to someone you are trying to communicate with. It creates angst or tension.

The other aspect of this is when you have texted a question to this other person and before you *barely* press "Send" and text them your communication, *they* send over *their* question.

Your irritation kicks in. You wanted an answer to *your* question!

Now you have their question or text. So do you answer it? Or blow it off and text them to answer *your original question?*

And because texting happens so quickly in a span of literally seconds, 3-5 texts can be sent back and forth without either of your original texts or questions being addressed.

And you wonder why there are Facebreaks.

The reason why this texting gets so irritating is that in real life you would not do what you do while you're texting. It's just really kind of silly. But then this is the virtual world and there is no Virtual World Handbook handed out to everyone with how to play or interact.

Somewhere early on in life we all developed the ability to communicate with someone else. It may have come naturally, or taught by our parents. You may have even taken a communications class or workshop to improve your skills in communicating.

And setting aside your own skills in communicating, most people know some basic fundamentals. Like the one you learned at the dinner table when you began to talk while your father was talking and your Mom looked at you and in a slightly admonishing tone said, *"Michael, do not talk while you're father is talking."* You took that well, because something in your makeup even as an eleven year-old, reminded *you knew* you weren't supposed to be talking.

To get a proper perspective of this, let's look at how this would appear if you were doing this in the real world.

First, just for fun, let's say you are in the kitchen with your husband. You're about ten feet away from each other. Between you and him there is a wall. And in the middle of that wall is a slot, like a mail slot. On his side and yours you both have a legal sized note pad and pen next to you. Now, you're not going to physically talk, because you don't do that on Facebook.

You want to ask him a question so you pick up your legal pad and start to write him a question. He's on the other side making a sandwich. You write out your question and push it through the mail slot. He looks over and notices it drop on the floor. He picks it up, reads it, sets it down and thinks on it for a minute while he finishes putting some lettuce on his sandwich. You, on the other side, are *wondering what in the name of geezus is taking him so long to write an answer?!* You begin to get *anxious.* You decide a *minute* is *waaaaaay too long* so you begin to write another question. But now on his side he picks up his pad and starts to write *his reply* and puts it in the mail slot to you just as you put your second note in to him.

You now have his reply which is <u>so</u> not the answer to your question.

Sometimes you wonder if your husband has a brain. You're more irritated. Now you need to get him to get his act together and answer your original question *for gawds sake.* So you start writing your next "text." He, on the other side is done with the first question and is reading the second one. He *senses* by the words you use in the second one that *you are beefed for some reason.* So he writes back, *"Stop acting like your Mom,"* and slides that on through. You now, are *mid* your *third* text and you stop as you see his next come through. You pick up his text and read it. You are *fuming.* You hate, I repeat *hate* when he brings your Mom into these things. You are now sure your husband must have not been in line when they passed out brains. You are so upset that you start writing your next text ALL IN CAPITAL LETTERS because *boy oh boy* you want him to know how mad you are and that you need to WRITE IN CAPITALS to reach that NEANDERTHAL LIZARD BRAIN OF HIS.

On the other side your husband figures his *"Stop acting like your Mom"* text will "put you in your place," finishes making his sandwich and takes a bite feeling quite kingly. As he's chomping down on his delicious man-creation he sees your next text come through. He picks it up and sees it's ALL IN CAPITAL LETTERS. And he doesn't actually *read* it really. He's so furious that you used CAPITAL LETTERS that he feels (and knows in the virtual world) that you are YELLING AT HIM and when you yell or raise your voice here in "text world" or in "real world" that *you are now off your rocker.* So he just rolls that text up into a tiny ball and "shoots it like a basketball" into the trash and yells out "Two points!"

Okay, well, if that isn't the definition of insanity I don't know what is.

But if you followed it, it's *exactly* what happens every hour of every day on Facebook.

And now we have a *Facebreak.*

And the problem that grew out of that exchange only gets bigger because on each side of that wall, completely outside of the virtual world of Facebook, both of you now have a *Facebreak.* You have a *real* breakdown in your communication. And that now has led to the both of you having an out of harmony relationship with each other. You now have this upset, this *"I cannot believe he said that"* frame of mind.

You also have all of the thoughts that have built up like a bad ant-hill in your mind about your husband that you go so far as to think *"Why the hell did I ever marry him?!!"* I mean your thoughts compound like bad banking interest. You try to chill. You have a glass of wine. You do some house work. While vacuuming you think of the "perfect" thing you are going to say to your husband when he gets home. You get more housework done than normal because, well...because you channel that fury from your *Facebreak* with that new Dyson he bought you.

Now let's check in with your husband. He's made "two points" with your silly-ass text because you're YELLING at him. He sits down and watches some football. As he watches the game he thinks that you are sometimes just bat-shit-crazy and now you'll probably not want to have sex with him tonight and he tries to just not worry about that because his favorite football team just scored and he's jumping off the couch cheering like some lunatic.

Okay, so here's deal: Let's go back to SOME kind of communication etiquette or manners. You know, like *don't talk while your father's talking.* Or you learned on a communication course that you communicate and finish, the other person acknowledges you that he heard you and understood you. He at least nods his head, "Okay, yeah, I got what you're saying about needing new curtains." You then feel *acknowledged*, you know? Like there's attentiveness to what you said. He didn't interrupt you when he heard you bring the "new curtains" phrase into the communication. You appreciated that. And then he replies with some decorum. You *know* this curtain issue gets him riled up, but he's not riled up. He's actually now returning a communication to you that's, well...that's *treating you as a person.* It's respectful. He's not riled up. He'd not mad. But he does have a legitimate question. And you are so appreciative that he isn't reacting and truly "being in communication with you," that you too, *listen*. You don't cut him off mid-sentence or interrupt him when his question has been asked.

Wow. A back and forth communication cycle. You talk. He acknowledges. He talks, you acknowledge. It works. Dad talks, you listen. Dad is opinionated and wrong, but you listen. You learned this from watching your Mom. Lord have mercy that woman had patience.

Exactly. Mom had patience and respect and understanding. She was a smart gal too. She knew your Dad was opinionated and he thought he was right all the time. She *knew* this. She knew this better than anyone. So how on god's green Earth did they get along?

Because they had some semblance of respect for the other. When your Mom spoke *he listened too*. He may have said, *"Now Mary, you've been reading too many romance novels,"* and she smiles and *knows this is how he is*. She doesn't get into a row about it.

Now this is just a snapshot of etiquette or manners. Mary and her husband are not perfect nor are you or I. And they will have their spats. But they've been married for 45 years and well, there is more sanity in the above exchange than most of what happens in many Facebook Messaging conversations. And the reason their model is better is that there was some foundation on how you communicate to another. They did not interrupt each other. They did not USE CAPITALS at the dinner table. They nodded and acknowledged. They went back and forth like a great set at Wimbledon.

And whether it's tennis or texting there are some understood rules.

And this is what each person or couple needs to work out when communicating. If you don't like the "bubble" coming up right when you are writing, just take a time out and say, "Hey, let me finish writing first." And don't *you* fire back, "Well type faster!"

See the speed of the virtual world has everyone all amped up because you want an answer *right now*. And if you take too long you are like some insensitive, slow moving, technology challenged hobo.

Stop with all the criticism and admonitions. Your Mom did it with class. You didn't feel made wrong or like you were reduced to the size of a pea.

Be.
More.
Like.
Mom.

If you examine any *Facebreak* you've had, I can guarantee it started with some violation of a common courtesy, etiquette, or manners we all learned about communicating early on in our lives.

When you wanted to speak in 3rd grade you raised your hand. You didn't just interrupt the teacher and speak. When she said, "Yes, Michael, you have a question?" *It worked.*

When you sit at the executive conference table and each of the executives has something to say, the CEO acknowledges each in turn and you speak. If there is a disagreement or the conversation gets heated between you and another colleague, the CEO jumps in and puts a halt to it. And just like Mom he says, *"Michael, I understand you're passionate about your project, but let Ed finish what he's saying. Hear him out."* You sit back in your chair and you think *Okay* and your mind goes back to Mom.

That's right.

Be. More. Like. Mom.

Chapter Four

When Did You Get Your Masters
in Psychoanalysis?

You just received a text from your partner or spouse.

You look down at the screen and it says, *"Why didn't you tell me we were out of milk?"*

You are in the middle of trying to finish a project at work and your husband who had a short day at work and was home early, probably wanted to make a protein shake as that's his favorite thing to do with milk.

You are behind in getting your proposal finished and you realize you cannot have your husband getting angry at you right now. Not now. Not when you have this important project to get done. You think as you re-read the text again that he has no reason to be mad at you because you were out of milk. To get this off your plate in *your* distempered state of mind you text back, *"There's no reason for you to be angry with me, if you need milk why don't you just go out and get some?"*

Now, before John receives this distempered text from you, he's at home feeling good. He's got the Rolling Stones turned up cranking out "Brown Sugar," and he's just happy as a lark because he closed a big deal, made a good commission and he's home early. Something that doesn't happen that often. He's just kind of footloose and fancy free walkin' around the kitchen getting some ingredients together to put some steaks on the grill for a dinner with you tonight.

John is not mad at all.

He just realized there was no milk and thought to dash off a text to you asking you why you didn't let him know you were out of milk. He thought if you did, he would've picked up some on the way home from work.

Enter the Armchair Psychologist.

This again is where many, *many Facebreaks* occur. People *"reading into"* what the tone, attitude or frame of mind of the person writing the text. Jennifer thought John was angry. She *"picked it up from the nature of his text."*

This is a *real gray area* that needs some light shined on it.

You can write a text in anger and tell someone *"I am really mad that you told Roger we weren't coming to their party. That soooo pisses me off."* See, that's just obvious by the language that one is mad.

But *"reading into"* a text can be dangerous. There is no class that you or anyone has taken that taught you or I how to *"read into"* a text.

Oh yes, we all think we're pretty perceptive about the tone of the text. We all think when we receive a text on our end that makes us feel a bit rankled, that *the person sending it was upset.* When we receive it like Jennifer above, sometimes (actually by survey more times than not) it was *your own tone or mood* that was part of the problem too.

Let's return to Jennifer and John.

So Jennifer, as you can see, has two situations occurring with her.

First, she's at work and she's in a frame of mind that is obviously a stressful one. I mean you could be a co-worker and approach her while she's hell-bent for leather on her computer and ask her *"Hey Jen... have you seen the Evans File?"* and she replies back rather curtly, *"Megan, I haven't got time right now---sorry---I've got to get this proposal done."* Megan can see you are in flat-out mode and turns right around and walks right out.

So Jennifer has her *own* mood. Something to note the next time you receive a text.

Secondly, Jennifer *reads into* John's text. *Was he mad? Did it sound mad?* I bet when you read it or re-read it as it is written above that you could chime in, "Well, it sounds like he might be mad."

Really?

What does mad "sound" like in a text?

Exactly.

There is no sound coming from John's text. There is only your perception or misperception of what the tone of John's text is.

And it is this *subtle but powerful* misperceived perception that then produces the billiard ball effect that is about to occur with John and Jennifer. And the reason this point is so important is that there is a *Facebreak* brewing from just what we have read so far about their situation.

Back to John and Jennifer.

Jennifer has sent her distempered text off. She probably intuitively knows she was not in the best of moods and probably shouldn't have sent that reply. See, you, Jennifer, me, we all know in that *billionth of second* that when we clicked the Send button, that it may not have been the best course of action. This is important to note because when it blows up, each person needs to take responsibility for *their* part in where this thing ends up. *So remember this point.* Like you learned as a kid. Count to five before you send that text. Examine your mood. In relationship to what is about to occur between Jennifer and John, it's a small discipline to learn that could save you enormous grief down the road.

Enter John.

John set his cell phone down on the kitchen island while he was lining up his steak supplies. Brown Sugar ended and now Alice Cooper's "School's Out for Summer" is blasting away. John is rocking away and hears the familiar "ping" of his cell phone. He stops his air guitar imitation and picks up his cell phone. He opens his text window and begins to read your text:

"There's no reason for you to be angry with me, if you need milk why don't you just go out and get some?"

Freeze frame.

If you follow John's state of mind and you read the above, what would you *assume* would be John's reaction? Good? Not so good?

Probably the latter.

The first line of text Jennifer sent not only *assumes* John is mad, the way she wrote it she actually *accuses* him of being mad. This will incense John because one, he's not mad and two Jennifer has no right to accuse him of being mad. It's one thing to get it wrong about his disposition, but to *accuse* him lights the match.

And then Jennifer pours gasoline on the fire. John *interprets the latter part of her text that she is now getting snotty with him.*

John hates snotty.

John's blood is boiling slightly here. He was having a damn good time and his wife has to get snotty with him. He is so pissed now he re-reads the test and gets more pissed. He's SURE now she's out of place with what she wrote.

Freeze frame.

When you are in a tone or mood that is distempered or embroiled, the natural reaction is to take your state of being embroiled and without really counting to five, you innately want to push back. You want to take this upset and tell the other person they are wrong or WTF?! or send some "zinger" back. If there is any wisdom from my years of counseling others that I can pass along to you here, it would be to take a moment to *stop and observe.* The world needs less zingers.

When you are consumed with that silent rage you often wish to send that rage back where it came from. It's completely and totally reactive and robotic. It's Pavlovian. It's silly and stupid and this now is going to get worse. You can see it here. And you can see this in your own life to whatever degree.

THE HARDEST THING TO DO WHEN YOU FEEL WRONGLY "STUNG" IS TO RESIST TRYING TO STING THE OTHER PERSON BACK.

But if you want to put more control and affinity in your relationships when these things come about, *resist the urge to strike back.*

So now we have John, who was *not* mad and was actually having a grand day of celebrating, now experiencing a shift in mood. He will feel like Jennifer's text *ruined his day.* It will come up later at dinner over an argument. That's how this thing snowballs.

So John is now upset. And he's in a *how-dare-you-ruin-my-day-with-your-snotty-attitude-text* mood. He knows better too. John's a bright guy. But he doesn't care. Like I said, he's embroiled. Like somebody cutting in front of you on the freeway and almost hitting you, you *almost* want to ram the dude who did that. So John's in the ramming mode. He then types out the following to Jennifer.

"Jen, where in the hell did you get the idea I was mad????
(John adds lots of ??? for effect). *You need to stop PMSing and knock off this bullshit. And btw, it's your job to keep groceries in the fridge. So how about you pick up some milk on your way home?"*

Whoa. John blew a gasket right there. He's after Jen big time. John even re-reads his text (you do this too) to ensure *he got it just right.* He needed to check and see if he needed to add any CAPS. Or throw in an emoji for effect. He looks it over, *and hits Send.*

DING, DING, DING... *"Laaaaadies and Gentlemennnn,* in the far corner wearing a grey Vera Wang business suit we have Jennifer Mills. And the opposite corner wearing a starch white Ralph Lauren business shirt with his tied loosened for comfort, we have John Mills.

At the sound of the bell, come out fighting!"

That's right. From the moment that Jennifer misinterpreted or misperceived the mood of John's text the fight was on. John receiving her text was the *"I'll meet you behind the school building,"* reply.

You can only imagine what Jennifer's response will be when she reads John's text, especially since she's under enormous stress at work and the sand in the hourglass at work is only getting smaller.

Jennifer looks up at the clock and hits print on her proposal and gets herself ready to take the proposal to her boss who's been waiting. She hears the printer engage and hears her phone "chime" that familiar chime she has set on her phone for her hubby. She is not even in a frame of mind to be clear enough to know what's going to come across that text. Her mental bandwidth has been completely absorbed by finishing the proposal. She vaguely remembers her reply to John and hopes he didn't get upset. She did it on the spur of the moment. She was already sorry she thought to herself. But John's usually understanding so hopefully he didn't take it wrong.

Freeze frame.

Whoa. Jennifer's totally hoping for a therapist's *dream*. That her distempered text was going to be received by her husband with some heart and smiley face emojis. Her disconnect from her responsibility in sending that text is now going to be magnified by the upset John's text is now going to carry.

She listens as the printer chugs out the proposal. She opens the text from John and reads it:

"Jen, where in the hell did you get the idea I was mad???? You need to stop PMSing and knock off this bullshit. And btw, it's your job to keep groceries in the fridge. So how about you pick up some milk on your way home."

Jennifer gets *completely enraged* by how John could be so juvenile and inconsiderate. She thinks, *"I'm here working my ass off and you're home just having a grand ole time and you text me this?!!"* That's what she's thinking. She is *really* mad now. She has no time for John's bullshit. She hears the printer stop and gathers up her proposal. She throws her cell phone into her purse and marches off to her bosses office. She is *fuming* underneath.

"PMSing..." she thinks to herself. *Fuck you, John. God I hate when he uses that term. He thinks every time I react I'm PMSing.* She sets her upset aside and sees her boss.

Fast forward to Jennifer driving home.

She is now completely dialed in to her upset with John. She intentionally does not stop and get milk just to *get back* at John. She is playing the scenario out in her mind as she drives. He will ask why and she will say that she "had a hard day" and "just forgot." John will think it's bullshit and call her on it.

Jennifer drives on madly working out the perfect "zinger" to get back at John. She is getting so worked up she thinks *"Whatever got into John today?" "Probably flirting with Annette at work."*

See?

This only gets worse. Jennifer is dubbing-in or imagining scenarios that have no basis in fact. John is doing the same. They are both caught in this obsessive-compulsive web known as their reactive or negative minds. There is a reason some Buddhists call it the "monkey mind" because their personal monkeys are jumping around like their cage is on fire. And neither has the discipline to *just shut it down.* I mean look at what I'm describing here. You have possibly gone through something similar to this. Some harmonic of it. The worst part is that this negativity is gaining an entire new life of its own.

This is no longer about the initial texts. No way Jose. This has escalated into a range war. It's like those stories you read of people who live next door to each other and one person adds an addition to their house blocking the view of the other. Range war. And then a legal fight through city council etc. Crazy.

And the thing about this is that text---words---*l-e-t-t-e-r-s like these here that you are reading,* were *misinterpreted*, to be something they were not.

I could write here: You Suck. And you could interpret my mood. When you do, just remember you heard no tone intonation except what you supplied in your mind. There was no sound track. There was no underscore. There was no exclamation point.

Two words: You Suck.

If you want to play Dr. Phil or be Dr. Ruth or whomever you will need to again take full responsibility for what your "diagnosis" is. You will need to own that you interpreted their text and own it fully. If you're wrong you need to own that too. You do not have a degree in "Reading Tone, Attitude, and Disposition of Text Messages."

And even if you guess right, *you are playing with fire.*

Jennifer guessed wrong. She did. She didn't own it. John responded poorly as well. Neither took responsibility for the errant spark flying off from the campfire. And now they are about to meet head on to a brush fire that will take over their evening.

An evening where John was going to barbecue steaks, make Jennifer's favorite salad, share their favorite wine while they celebrated his success at the office.

That scenario is changing and will morph into something entirely different as Jennifer pulls up to the driveway at her house.

Don't be an Armchair Psychologist. Don't think because of your education or degrees that you are Dr. Phil or anyone that makes a living psychoanalyzing people.

Psychoanalysis reportedly has the highest suicide rate of any profession on the planet. Why enter *that* arena? It's suicide.

Be yourself. Keep your cool. Understand words can be inflammatory.

They are just words. Remember that. **You** are bigger than words.

Ah geezus. I just re-read what I wrote above where it said: You Suck.

Goddang autocorrect. Don't you just hate that?!!!!

It was *supposed* to say:

YOU *ROCK*.

Chapter Five

How 'Bout We Talk in a Broom Closet? LOL!

Did you ever stop and think about what we are *really* doing
when we are trying to have a *"conversation"* via iMessaging,
using Facebook's Messenger, or just your normal texting?

To start with, when you type in that little text space the space
itself is only two inches long and approximately a half inch
wide.

That's roughly about a third the size of a stick of bubblegum.

And in *that* space you get to type including spaces, an average of *about thirty characters.*

For those who don't immediately understand characters, the following sentence shows how much you get to write:

The quick brown fox jumped ove

That's it. That's how much you get to type to have this *"conversation."*

Couldn't even finish the word *over.*

I'm illuminating this because we forget where we came from. We came from sitting around campfires *having conversations.* At a local pub or bar sitting next to someone. At a church social or picnic. It was just the natural order of things.

Now you go to a campfire or a picnic and it is the weirdest thing ever.

Practically everyone is sitting around staring at their cellphone screen! *Whooooooeeee-yessireee,* we're having a conversation now!

Not.

Okay, so back to the physical space. You and I are going to have a conversation in a space less than the length of your little finger and half as wide. And we only get to type in about thirty characters to converse.

Meet you in the broom closet?

The fact is we were all brought up to have conversations in person until the advent of the telephone. In person, you didn't have a space limit. You could be standing two feet apart sharing a glass of wine. Or next to each other eating a bowl of cereal. Or your partner or colleague could be across the room and you could, and did, carry on a *conversation.* And the space did not limit how many words you could say. You just spoke. You could tell the other person, "Listen Bob, I have an idea I want to run by you," and Bob would nod, knowing what's coming is not thirty characters but an *idea.* He understands innately that the idea you are about to express will possibly be long---not too long--but enough to get your idea expressed. Space. Understanding.

It works.

And even on the phone you could talk to your heart's content. The phone did not beep when you had spoken too much. There was no timer. Again you didn't need to be conscious of how many words you used. You spoke. The other person listened. It went back and forth.

It was called having a conversation.

Conversation was allowed to flow back and forth whether over a glass of wine two feet apart, with a colleague over a conference table, or two teenage girls chatting away via Ma Bell and a phone line each on the other side of town.

Not until the advent of computers and email did this whole idea of having a conversation take on a new slant.

Even in email, as noted in the previous chapter, conversation was (and is) susceptible to *misunderstanding.* We've all written and received these kinds of emails.

Greg: "I got your email Wendy. You totally missed my point."

Wendy: WTF???

There is probably no worse feeling than being told *after* you wrote and often *crafted* an email that you *"totally missed my point."* And...oh...btw, that basically you were **twit** or **numbskull.** And the bad thing is the email was written *before* you went to bed, so you didn't receive the response until you got to work the next day.

How's that start your day?

You wanna text Jennifer and create an Alliance? Just make sure when you text her that you make a point to TEXT EVERYTHING IN CAPITALS AS TO WHAT ABSOLUTE JERKS THESE GUYS ARE. And throw in a mean face emoji just to stoke the fire.

Having a Conversation vs. Texting

Do you know the definition of texting? You could probably wing it and get close. I winged it *and* looked it up. Interesting.

SMS (Short Message Service), *commonly referred to as "text messaging," is a service for sending short messages of up to 160 characters*

Text messaging: *the sending of short text messages electronically especially from one cell phone to another. (Merriam Webster.)*

Okay so look. SMS---did you know what this meant? It's a Short. Message. Service. Notice the word **Short** modifies the word **Message.**

A short message. *Are we having a conversation?*

"Billy, give this message to Mom when you see her at the Parent Teacher meeting tonight. I'll be there shortly." Billy's dad hands Billy this note/message he wants Billy to give to his wife. *A short message.*

When you call someone on their cellphone and get their voicemail, do you leave them a conversation? Like do you ramble on about your idea or plan or whatever you wanted to talk about?

No. You leave them a *short message.*

We have all learned as the technology has advanced that we adjusted to the medium in relationship to our communication. When we no longer had to find a legal size notepad but could use a Post-It note, we put those all over our desktop or on the counter to remind us---leave ourselves a ***short message*** *to pick up some milk on the way home.*

And when voicemail came along we quickly adapted. *"Leave me a message at the beep."* *Beeeeeeep.* "Hey Mike, it's Dave. It's 2:15. Give me a call when you are free."

You were hoping to talk to Mike and *have a conversation* but you couldn't so you left him a *short message.*

SHORT MESSAGES ARE NOT CONVERSATIONS. THEY ARE SHORT MESSAGES.

As the technology has continued to advance we went to 140 characters on Twitter. We started having "thumbs up" icons on Facebook or a heart on Instagram to show we liked something.

But here we are in this space less than the size of your little finger, where you are *supposed to try and have a conversation.*

It may just be that when that tiny two inch text space appeared and you could text away you felt you *could* have a conversation. Well in the beginning when you sent, "Hi Bob, how's it going?" and he texted back, "Hey Dave, it's going really well. The Chiefs are winning!" Okay, that is a conversation. So I'm *not* trying to shut down that a conversation can't take place in a text message. What I'm trying to tell you that *it **wasn't built*** for conversations.

It was built as a Short. Message. Service.

This is what has happened in this text space: With the increase of and ease of use, including Swype type keyboards, etc, you can type faster and you *think* you can have a conversation.

You try to squeeze in communicating to your wife why you won't be home for dinner. And she's like WTF? And she's furiously typing back and neither of you can beat those bad-boy tiny pale gray ellipses bubbles that are chirping away as you both try to *"have this conversation."*

You are not going to handle a conversation that takes space and time and appropriate acknowledgements in two inches of space. You will try. No matter what I say here you will. And some of you will stubbornly tell me you do just fine. I don't disagree. But if you step back and understand what the original purpose of SMS was Facebook's iMessage (see---message) it was to *deliver a message.*

If you keep this in mind and use texting to deliver short messages or communications, i.e. "Honey, Megan's soccer game has been moved to 4:30 p.m. Just FYI," *you will do just fine.*

But if you think that sending your boyfriend a message like, *"I saw you put a heart next to Cathy Richardson's post. What's that all about?"* you are opening yourself up to a drive on a very icy road. Just pretend you're the boyfriend and you received *that* text. The girl, let's call her Sally, is *expecting* an explanation. She's not expecting a *short message.* If Michael texted back a short message, "I like her waterfall pictures," *that isn't going to cut it with Sally.* In fact the short message from Michael will only create upset with Sally because she's expecting an *explanation.* In context to what Sally is disturbed about, Michael's answer does not **a)** answer her question and **b)** by its cryptic nature, will *infuriate* Sally.

I hope you can see the error Sally is making. She is *not* in error for *asking* her question. But she is in error to use a Short. Message. System. and **expect and explanation** from Michael and or to carry out a conversation in a space a third of the size of stick of bubble gum.

And Michael is a fool if he thinks some short cryptic answer is going to somehow make Sally feel warm and fuzzy.

SALLY'S QUESTION IS BAD ENOUGH. BUT MICHAEL'S RESPONSE WILL BE THE MATCH THAT IGNITES A FIRESTORM.

Acronyms:

Years ago when I first saw someone put LOL at the end of their text I was like, *"Are you really on the other end laughing out loud?"* I mean *really?*

Many of you reading this (depending on your generation) might not think much of this because it seems like LOL and other acronyms have been around all the time. Well, obviously they weren't. Back in the early 80's when they came on the scene they were new. There were other meanings too, like "Lots of Love." So WTF, right? See?

Anyway, acronyms have their place and certainly with the small amount of space for texting, LOL fits much better than writing out *"laughing out loud."*

But always keep in mind that this acronym language fits the Wild West metaphor I've been using. It's loose. You can just pull your gun out and fire away LOL, LMAO, and ROFL. You know just an aside here. I was good with LMAO, but when it went to ROFL, I was like okay, no one's rolling on the floor laughing. And even if one didn't obviously interpret that literally, I just have never myself experienced *anything* so funny I would roll on the floor laughing. But maybe you have. Okay, score one for you. That's totally cool.

But my point is that the acronyms can begin to morph into this language that seems surreal. One time I was texting a woman back in 2009 and after just about every text she'd put LOL!!!

My whole relationship with her was changing with each LOL. If I met her in real life (which I never did) we'd be at a party or mixer talking and literally after about every two sentences she would be laughing out loud. If you can get that visual, that would mean that woman was a nut-job, right?! I mean check this out:

Me: *"Hi Cindy, how's it goin?"*
Cindy: *"Oh it's going good. I broke my high heel walking up the steps to get to this mixer though! LOL!"*
Me: *"I see. Well what do you think of the band tonight?"*
Cindy: *"I'm not that much into Alternative Rock but the lead singer is real cute! LOL"*
Me: (Okay that's two LOL's now and I'm like oooookaaaayyyy). *"So did your team get the project done by the deadline today?"*
Cindy: *"Damm it was close. But we just said WTF and threw that baby together! LOL!"*

Get my drift?

It gets *creepy-crazzzzeee* when there are so many LOL's you think you're talking to Chucko the Clown.

So this whole acronym is just something to be aware of not because you like to use them, *but remember the other person on the other end.* They may just think you are *whacked* with all your LOL and LMAO and ROFL.

Emojis:

Okay so let's get down and dirty about emojis.

It's just wild that these little emoticons or emojis can cause so much havoc. And they do.

Let's start with the homewrecker: The heart emoji. OMG. (Hey, check me out. I'm using OMG. You think I'm whacked? No probs. I totally know I am).

So you send or click the "heart" emoticon to a member of the opposite sex when you are in a relationship and you might as well be sticking your tongue down their throat.

The survey answers in this area were just filled with jealousy and hurt and truly have caused a rift or real upset in relationships.

Think about it for a minute. And let's go back to the mixer in the *real world.*

Jim: *"Hi Megan. You look nice this evening."*
Megan: *"Awwww. Thanks, Jim. That's so nice of you. Is your wife with you tonight?"*
Jim: *"No, Amy wasn't feeling well so it's just me."*
Megan: *"Oh, sorry to hear that. Hope she's feeling better."*

41

Jim: *"I'm sure she'll be fine. She's a trouper. By the way I noticed you did highlights in your hair. It really looks good on you. HERE LET ME GIVE YOU THIS RED HEART I HAVE IN MY POCKET BECAUSE I LIKE THE WAY YOU LOOK."*

I mean this IS what is occurring on Facebook or texting with your cell phone. You gotta look at this.

Let's say Jim's wife Amy *was* there at the mixer and she was across the room talking to an old friend named Susan. She's chatting away with Susan and looks over at you momentarily because her FEMALE RADAR IS GOING OFF BECAUSE JIM IS TALKING TO A VERY ATTRACTIVE YOUNGER WOMAN. Amy just "happens" to glance over as you HAND MEGAN THE HEART FROM YOUR POCKET.

Okay, so Pop Quiz: *What is Amy going to think when she sees her husband gushing at Megan and passing her a small heart into her hand? Hmmmm???*

That's right. (And here we go Acronym People). She's going to be like *WTF???*

So Megan thanks Jim for the heart and goes off with one of her girlfriends to socialize at the mixer. Jim is just looking around feelin' pretty good having chit-chatted with Megan. And then out of the corner of his eye he sees Amy finishing talking to this other woman and she starts walking over to Jim. Jim can tell from thirty feet away that there's a heat-seeking missile coming out of Amy. *Ah shit.* Jim gathers himself. Amy comes up to Jim smiling. Here's the convo:

Jim: *"Hi honey, who was that you were talking to?"*

Amy: *"Oh, that was Susan. Remember she was the one who I was talking about the other night who was looking for someone to walk with her in the 5K coming up in two weeks."*
Jim: (Jim barely remembers but feigns he does). *"Oh yes, uh huh.*
Amy: *"And who was that brunette you were talking to?*

Freeze frame.

See Amy doesn't say, "Say, who was that woman you were talking to, someone from work?" No. Amy uses *brunette.*

Okay get back to the convo.

Amy: *"And who was that brunette you were talking to?"*
Jim: (*Gulp*) *"Oh, that's Megan from Project Development. I was just talking with her about getting the project done by deadline today."*

Freeze frame.

Jim thinks, *he thinks* he can run that by Amy and have her buy it. The sphincter valves on his butt are tightening up hoping, *hoping* that that will be that about his little *chit-chat* with Megan. ROFL!

See? I'm just not going to use those anymore.
LMAO! Enough.

So Jim knows, and you know, and your spouse knows because we all have this kind of innate sixth-sense about these things even though we sometimes don't use it, right? I mean Jim knows he's trying to throw a slider at the knees at Amy to get the ump to call strike and tell her to *get outta here.*

Not so fast, Jim.

You're about to get that heat-seeking missle question from Amy you were hoping to dodge. It's like your whole future is moving in slow-motion now. You are just ever-so-slightly perspiring. Here it comes and your sphincter valves are as about as tight as they can be.

Amy: *"Oh, that's nice. And I happened to see you hand her a heart. What was that all about?"*

Fucking Freeze Frame Right Now.

Okay so let's get the visual:

Amy is standing right next to her husband Jim, looking up at him and he down at her. They have been married for 12 years. They love each other. They have their moments, but they have worked through their issues. And Jim is feeling guilty now. Even just a *bit.* Maybe giving Megan the heart because she looked pretty went *too* far. But hey, *maybe not* you know? He wasn't having *sex* with her. And she *was* pretty. *And what the hell?* He just gave her a heart which meant *he really liked how she looked.* Nice try Jim. Stop with the whole justification and rationalization thing. And *plaaaeeeesseee* don't sell that to Amy. Just. Don't. Do it.

And Amy saw that he *liked* Meagan with the heart. There's Amy scrolling through Facebook and she sees that Jim has hearted Megan's picture. And Amy *also* thinks: *My god*

Megan is beautiful. Amy thinks about the wrinkles just starting to come around *her own* eyes. She thinks about her tummy that's not like it used to be in college. She introverts slightly. She's also trying to give her husband the benefit of the doubt. I mean he just liked her picture. Don't take those French nails and slash them across his face. Yet.

Back to the convo:

Amy: *"Oh, that's nice. And I happened to see you hand her a heart. What was that all about?"*

Freeze frame again.

Unfortunately, after four decades of counseling couples they don't always come clean right off the bat. That's also in our inherent ancestral human memories. You know, you take the cookie out of the cookie jar when you weren't supposed to and your Mom calls you out on it. You have some chocolate chips smudges on your hands and you are ever-so-slightly squirming. And your Mom asks you that heat-seeking missle question:

"Billy, did you steal a cookie out of the cookie jar?"

Another *"Gulp"* moment.

I mean we *did* it. You *did* it. We know *we did it.* But what did we say in most cases? *"No, not me."*

Here is my new acronym for Billy and Jim and all of us who have been there done that with that answer: IASS!

I AM SO STUPID.

Jim is about to have an IASS Moment. It's actually painful to watch.

But here we go…

Jim: *"Oh, ah..you know, she did her hair* (OMG Jim you're blowing it! Do. Not. Mention. Another. Woman's. Hair!) *a different way than usual and I really thought she looked nice and so I liked her picture with a heart."*

Amy: Amy at this point just looks at her husband. It's gone quiet like after a car accident in the movies and she's wandering around lost. You see everyone yelling and screaming and it's all in slow motion but there is no sound. *Amy is in this no sound moment.* All she hears is *"she did her hair…"* and then she just zoned out. And she is just kind of in shock you know. Like when the policeman comes up to her and asks, *"Are you okay?"* And Amy sees the policeman's lips moving and he's very concerned but *she doesn't hear anything.*

Except *"she did her hair a different way…"*

Okay so now all of a sudden the sound comes back on for Amy and she hears the voices at the mixer and people having a good time. She's looking up at her husband and he at her and they just both kind of know they're in this **awkward moment.** I'm not sure there's a better description for this moment because, well, because it is just ***friggin' awkward.*** How do you define this moment really? If you're going to psychoanalyze Jim or pass judgment good luck with that. If

Amy tries to pretend it didn't affect her or push further she knows that *does not* work either.

See there's this sanctity in their marriage that every so often takes these random hits. They seemingly come out of the blue like tonight. And they are somewhat innocuous *but they are not*. And there is no right answer. If Jim really did like her because she's beautiful that's not going to go down well. If he tries to pull back on that and color it like it's "no big thing" that will not go down well either. See?

Awkward.

And Amy knows her husband likes pretty women. And she *knows* he loves her. But those two things don't sit well from somewhere deep within her female DNA either. Especially because she knows that Megan is physically more beautiful than her. And it makes Amy think about her age. And this whole thing is just one big friggin' hornet's nest.

So time out.

Here we have two people who love each other and have somehow done the superhuman feat of staying together for 12 + years. Anyone who is married who is reading knows this is truly a great report card.

But the tough thing with these moments is when we bring them back to the world of texting and Facebook emoji's you once again are playing with fire. In the mixer example it's right out there for Jim to do and Amy to see. With texting it's more secretive and covert. And often because of *that very reason* it seems more clandestine and hidden and something like the little kind lying about stealing the cookie. And when Amy sees you "Liked" Megan or sent her a heart emoji she enters the Twilight Zone, really. She is straddling the invisible line because she knows somewhere deep inside her that this is not the end of the world but it sure feels like *this is how the end of the world starts.* She knows if she tries to make something more of it or ask too many probing questions that she makes her own case worse. And having done that very thing in the past she knows Jim gets more and more riddled that she is "making it such a big deal" and yet she can't get him to see that it *is* a big deal. It's big enough that they both look at each other and hope that what just occurred here won't break that sanctity that is their marriage. Because somewhere deep within their own souls they know how much work it took to get this far and doing something like this could in fact fracture that which they hold so sacred.

Amy looks away with the far off look like she's looking for Megan. Jim only stares at his wife because he knows. He knows that he stole a bit of her heart giving that much attention to Megan. And he takes another sip of his drink and thinks to himself:

IASS!

Chapter Six

Sharing Pics of Your Exes:
Please Put on Your Hazmat Suit

Have you ever sat on your couch with your partner and you both have your cell phones and you are on Facebook surfing and sharing YouTube videos or pictures you like?

And then your girlfriend asks you what your ex-girlfriend looks like?

Freeze the friggin' frame *right now*.

I will probably use the word *innocuous* too many times in this book but it is the *appropriate* word.

WARNING: SHARING PICS OF EX'S: IT SEEMS INNOCUOUS. STEP AWAY FROM YOUR CAR AND PUT YOUR HANDS ABOVE YOUR HEAD. I AM WRITING THIS IN CAPS AND ALSO USING A BULLHORN. DO YOU HEAR THE BULLHORN? DO. NOT. DO. THIS.

It is *not* innocuous. It may *feel* innocuous. It is *not*. It might *sound* innocuous. *It. is. not.*

WARNING: DO NOT FALL FOR YOUR GIRLFRIENDS PLAYFUL TONE OF VOICE OF "LETS SEE LETS SEE COME ON!"AS SHE LEANS OVER TO PEER AT YOUR PHONE. YOU ARE ABOUT TO DO SOMETHING WORSE THAN SHAKE A CONTAINER OF PLUTONIUM.

It is so far from innocuous it's not funny. And soon, very soon it will not be funny at all.

This scenario showed up countless times in my surveys. Both sexes showing the other pictures of their exes.

Let's take a real life couple who answered the survey. Their names will be changed because holy cow they would shit if I didn't.

Let's take the example of Greg and Samantha.

Okay, so Greg goes up to his browser and types in the name of his ex-girlfriend: *Michele Richards.*

Up comes her Facebook profile.

Here's the very first thing that Greg's girlfriend will see:

HOW BEAUTIFUL MICHELE IS. THAT'S WHAT SHE SEES.

And even if she gets over that, (which she really doesn't entirely). Samantha just did the opposite of what her own intuition told her not to do: Look at the woman that *you* were with *before* her.

Samantha's mind right now is doing what only some IBM Supercomputers can do: She is looking at every tiny little thing about that profile picture of Michele and in an instant of super-lightning-fast computing *she is sizing her up as compared to her.* If Michele is younger *good luck.* If Michele is naturally beautiful *good luck.* And if she's sexy well...all I can tell you is that your girlfriend's synapses are now misfiring and she's actually, deep *deep* down in her secret heart-of-hearts, *regretting she asked you.* But for some *primordial* reason she eggs you on to scroll through Michele's pictures so she can see more. Most likely to see if Michele is fat. Or see her with her new boyfriend. Or look for wrinkles. Or *something.*

And then the worst case scenario happens. That's right, you guessed it.

On Michele's personal page as Greg is scrolling down is a picture of *Greg and Michele in Hawaii.* Michele is *not* fat. In fact Michele looks *friggin' fantastic* in her bikini. And she's got her arms draped around Greg giving him a big kiss on the cheek.

And in the picture Greg is glowing like Don Ho on steroids.

Freeze frame.

Okay what just happened here in this millisecond with Greg when he came upon this picture of him and Michele in Hawaii?

Let's inspect this while we've got this thing frozen in time.

Enter Greg.

So Mr. Okay-I'll-go-along-with-your-giggles-and-grins-Samantha and show you a pic of my ex.

Oops.

Oops doesn't even *begin* to describe what is happening in this precise moment of time. This is bigger than Oops. This is *OopsFuckinOops* to the max. Further known as **OFO** from here forward.

You have "stumbled upon" THE EXACT WRONG PICTURE for this cozy little fun fest happening on the couch with your girlfriend Samantha.

When you scroll down and see this picture, let's take a closer look at all the various thoughts and emotions going through that male brain of yours, shall we?

You see this pic and *dammmmnnnnn* does Michelle look good in that bikini! **OFO**. And she *does* have a *hot* body. And you fast forward in your lizard-brain mind of yours to the outrageous sex you and Michele had that evening. **OFO x100.**

And you also notice how big that shit-eating grin of yours is while Michele's planting that nice smooch on your cheek. You've never been that tan in your life and that million dollar smile looks like... well it looks like a *million* dollars. And just in the millisecond you see all of this, you **get one more perception** that totally interrupts your stroll down memory lane: You can sense the shock and dismay from Samantha as she sits next to you. Your reverie in the pleasure moment of that picture crashes like you're coming off some heroin high and your heart sinks and you feel like this was the most stupidest thing you could have ever done. Did I say innocuous? *Yes, I believe I did.*

Did I not give you a WARNING???!!! Hmmmmmmm??

Well Mr. I-Just-Did-The-Most-Stupidest-Thing-Ever, you are now going to get *another* warning. And that's when I remove this Freeze Frame and we go over to Samantha's world in real time.

WARNING: DO NOT PRETEND YOU CAN UNDERSTAND WHAT SAMANTHA IS EXPERIENCING RIGHT THIS MINUTE. DO NOT EVEN TRY.

WARNING: DO NOT "WATER DOWN" WHAT IS GOING ON IN THIS HAWAII PICTURE WITH YOU AND MICHELE. WOMEN ARE NOT STUPID. ESPECIALLY AT MOMENTS LIKE THIS. THEY ARE IN FACT SAVANTS. THEY ARE CLAIRVOYANT. WHAT'S GOING ON IN THIS PICTURE IS OBVIOUS. IT'S OBVIOUS TO YOU. IT'S OBVIOUS TO HER. IT WOULD BE OBVIOUS TO GUMBY.

Okay, here we go...back to real time...

Samantha sees this picture of you and Michele and remember that IBM Supercomputer I spoke of earlier? You know the millions of computations that it can do? That is what is going on with Michele's brain right now. Did I say millions? Sorry. I misspoke. It's more like:

A GAZILLION.

And that gazillion includes every range of emotion a woman can feel in a *millisecond*. And the thoughts she's thinking about that picture, and you, and you and Michele, and the setting, *and, and and...* well her emotional thought synapses are burning out like a bad grid blackout in New York.

And you FEEL ALL OF THIS from Samantha. And it's friggin' weird, *right?*

And this is why this is in fact not innocuous. More like _noxious._

This seemingly "innocent" and fun play you guys were having like five minutes ago on your couch laughing and sharing pics has slid into this ALTERNATIVE UNIVERSE. That's right. Sulu pushed FULL WARP SPEED AHEAD and all that laughing and giggling you were just doing? That universe is GONE. GONE-GONE. You are still sitting on the same couch. You are still there right next to each other. But this is just like putting on Virtual Reality Goggles. You are in another world right now.

And truth be told?

Neither of you know how to navigate this world.

And the oddest thing happens next before you can say WTF???

Do you know what Samantha does?

She takes your phone out of your hands and looks even closer at the picture of you and Michele!

Is there an acronym for this? Hmmmmm...Okay...I will make one:

NWTIHTM!

NO WAY THIS IS HAPPENING TO ME.

WAY.

Yes it is happening and it's happening at breakneck speed. Greg is feeling really uncomfortable right now. He also has a million thoughts going through his mind. Like how Michelle is a psycho-chick and that she spends way too much time looking in the mirror and that she uses the word *"seriously"* way *way* too much like she was some throw back to the Valley Girls. After a while Greg didn't even like the sex because she was...well...*she was whacked.*

So Greg contemplates as those milliseconds are speeding by to tell Samantha all this. **Warning:** Greg man, listen up. Do. Not. Tell. Her. You. Didn't. Like. The. Sex. No matter if you had sex with a female gorilla a woman does not want to hear about it. Zero. Zippo. Nada.

Houston: *"This is Houston to Apollo 13, do you see this clearly? Over."*

Greg: *"Houston this is Captain Greg Ramirez. Copy that. Over."*

I am so glad you copy that Greg. You still are about to experience some collateral damage so buckle up.

Enter Samantha:

Samantha now has Greg's cell phone and is looking over this picture of Greg and Michele. In fact she's looking at it like she owned a photo lab and had one of those eyepieces in her eye and inspecting that one picture for any blemishes or grainy impressions. But she's not looking at the quality of the picture or for too much pixelation. Samantha has got that eyepiece squarely going over every inch of Michele. Maybe hoping to find some cellulite or some (ugly?) quirk. And all the while she's doing the "inspection" her actual feelings are turning inward on her. The original playful tone and "LET'S SEE LET'S SEE!" has long disappeared and now she is confronting several mixed emotions including the most deadly for Samantha:

Comparing herself to Michele.

Samantha finishes her inspection and is feeling like she never should have bitten into that forbidden apple. Yes, the *allure of temptation.* The invisible line going off silently just before she steps out into the crosswalk flashing "DON'T WALK." But she's a big girl and she looked both ways and *still* walked right into the oncoming traffic that is now flooding her mind, her heart, and her soul. The emotions themselves are overwhelming. And Samantha freezes right there.

Freeze Frame.

What is going on in Samantha's world could be a whole book itself. When she answered the survey you could tell the hurt that occurred. I could tell by her answers she was a bright gal. She articulated her experience well. But she's a woman. And women feel with more depth than men from my experience as a counselor. And you could just tell. She thought it was *all going to be playful fun.* And it was. But then she crossed that invisible line and stepped out into the oncoming traffic of emotions and thoughts that were, in fact, *overwhelming.* She wasn't expecting this. Of course. Had she known, she would have heeded the silent red flashing "DON'T WALK" sign.

But here she is. And I want to pass her experience onto you so that whether man or woman, you get a glimpse and possibly some understanding of the ramifications of doing these seemingly *"innocuous"* things.

First of all, Samantha loves Greg. *She loves her man to death.*

But seeing Greg with another woman was like someone momentarily shooting her with a Taser Gun. And see, Greg had told her early on in his relationship about Michele and what a psycho-chick she was. They had a good laugh about it- --*back then.*

Well if a picture is worth a thousand words, this picture of *Greg and Michele* in Hawaii is blowing the circuits on words in Samantha's mind. And here's what's important: When Samantha got the *full visual* of Michele WITH Greg, *she didn't know what to do or say.*

Samantha found herself in the nebulae of a world where her brain could not assimilate what was in fact occurring. She was at once very cognizant of the fact that *she* was the one that asked Greg...no...*she playfully insisted* that they look at his ex. So she knew she stepped out into the crosswalk on her own determinism. Yet at the same time, she was reeling from the fact that this other woman, Greg's ex, was extremely attractive. And because she also knew how much Greg enjoyed sex, she could not keep her mind from straying into that airspace as well.

Samantha admitted that although she made it seem like it didn't bother her when talking with Greg at the time, she was actually very honest in her answers in the survey that it *did* bother her. And that for a while she couldn't shake it. She realized that that picture and her own imagination of them together followed her particularly when they were in bed together. And this became the wake-up call for Samantha. She decided that what she had with Greg was something special and that she was going to protect that going forward. She realized the past is the past and Greg *did not* have eyes for another woman, that this was not about Greg or other women.

This was about her own personal integrity to herself and the integrity of the relationship she was in.

We talked about integrity in Chapter 2. In her own way she evolved the same idea that it was better to not wade into those waters under the guise of fun and just "playing around."

It was not fun in the end and so she'd decided she'd rather be playful with Greg in other ways and leave this Twilight Zone to Rod Serling re-runs.

Greg and Samantha did not break up by the way. Not from what I could tell from the survey. But they both answered because they felt that other couples should know that there is a lesson to be learned:

That instead of learning the hard way and feeling the hurt, that when you see the silent red "DON'T WALK" sign, realize even when there *seems to be no traffic,* ("you're just having fun") the "DON'T WALK" sign *was put there for a reason.*

It wasn't there to police you or forbid you. But to warn you that by crossing right now would not be such a good idea.

And yeah. In the end that's what we want to ask ourselves, *right?*

Is this a good idea to go look at our exes or not?

Chapter Seven:

Artificial Intimacy, Secrets, and Hide n' Go Seek

Hide: *to conceal from sight; prevent from being seen or discovered.*

(Merriam Webster)

I want to talk about *hiding*. Interesting word. Curious concept.

Admit it. At some point in your life, you've hidden something from your partner, boss, friends, family, or someone close to you.

Hiding!

And I also and going to broaden this concept of hiding because in the Facebook World, there is a tendency to not just hide things you are doing, but also per the definition above, *"...prevent from being seen or discovered."*

Now this chapter might make you squirm a little. Or a lot!

It's okay, because see there is no one walking this planet that hasn't hidden some secret, some magazine, some piece of clothing, some note, some email, some price tag, something bought, or even something stolen.

We. Are. All. Busted.

You good with that? You're not going to go all righteous on me and write a review that says that this is poppycock, right?

Who uses the word *poppycock* anyway?

Okay, back to hiding…

So call this the I-know-you-hide-you-know-I-hide-and-we-know-others-hide-too chapter and just be cool, okay? I won't be telling on you.

The thing about hiding is so ridiculous, actually.

One time I was working with a client trying to prove a point. I asked him to take the keys out of his pocket and then look around the room and hide them where he couldn't find them. You read that right. Where *he* couldn't find them.

He actually looked around the room to where he might hide them.

True story.

And not before, but near a couple of scans around the room the embarrassed smile came over his face. *Exactly!* You can't really hide anything from yourself because *you know where you put it.*

So rule #1 is that even if you are hiding something from another, you are first buying into *the whole idea you can hide.*

Yet even good ol Merriam-Webster tells us in the definition of hiding that you are trying to "*...conceal something from sight.*"

It's just friggin' ridiculous.

Conceal something from sight?

So...ummm...*sight* can find it, but you have to *conceal* it from sight *so it won't.*

Have I got that right?

So this is like Hide n' Go Seek, right?

I mean you're not *destroying* the Playboy magazine as an amped-up hormone firing teenage boy or the price tag from your $350 Vera Wang blouse while you shopped at Nordstroms. And you're not *vaporizing* that secret note your co-worker passed over to you, right? And you're not *burning* that shirt or those panties that have evidence of some kind of shenanigans were going on. *Right?*

I just want to make sure we're all on the same page.

So we don't *destroy, vaporize,* or *burn* something we don't want another to see. But we will *conceal* it. I see.

Hmmmm..

Conceal it how?

You mean when you are perusing those women exercise videos with the sound turned down and your wife SEEMINGLY APPEARS OUT OF NOWHERE and asks you if you know where the Windex bottle is and when she gets to about *Win* in Windex you nervously click off and over to your Fantasy Football site.

You mean that kind of conceal?

And oh by the way; if you read Chapter 5, you recall that women are fucking CLAIRVOYANTS, right? So your whole "I'll instantly-click-off those-nice-tight-yoga-butt-videos-to-fantasy-football" nonsense is picked up BEFORE she even got *Windex bottle* out of her mouth.

Conceal?

Man you need to go all *Star Trek Cloaking Device* if you're going to conceal from your partner or spouse.

Let's get back to *ridiculousness.*

Because we're adults now and the notion that we need to conceal from sight is...well...to be honest...*is slowing destroying the intimacy and trust in most relationships.*

Reading the survey answers was quite the reality adjustment. It's like Alice falling down the rabbit hole. She sees the Red Queen and Red King and comes back to tell you secretly that they were having sex in the forest outside the kingdom walls. And you're like, *WTF?* And then you really just think it's all made up.

Except it isn't.

The fact is that individuals and couples go online every day and they go down the rabbit hole and are just wowed by all that's there. And when it gets boring, *you look for more wow.*

If you're a woman and you like some guy's picture you click on it. In your own little space and time, you check him out. Could be a co-worker. Could be a friend. And you're married. Or in a serious relationship. But hey, you're not doing anything wrong. *Right?*

Well let's just say your husband or partner popped in like Barbara Eden did on I Dream of Genie. You know, just *PING!* And your husband is sitting right next to you while you gawk at this picture of this guy.

"Lucy, you got some 'splaining to do."

Well let's just let Barbara Eden *PING* away and get back to you and your interest in this guy. See, it usually doesn't stop at just the profile pic, right? I mean there's the About button and there are Photos. Mmmmmm…more photos of Rick? You mean there's a *whole carton* of chocolate chip ice cream in the freezer?

Well it's just about the same. You cannot sit on that couch or in your home office knowing that there's *more*, and not investigate *the more.*

I mean when you go to the freezer and grab a spoon "just to take a few bites" of that delicious chocolate chip ice cream, how many times did you just practically finish that baby off?

Well, now you decide to go look at more pictures of Rick.

But something starts to enter your emotional bloodstream besides the excitement of possibly seeing him shirtless or lifting weights. Now it feels like you are spying on Rick. You immediately dismiss this word "spy" because that's for the CIA and the Man from Uncle. Nah. You're just *curious*. Like Alice. Okay, that makes you feel better.

You're Alice.

But Alice was an imaginary character and you are having a bit of real guilt turn on. You ignore this. *Where are those half-naked six-pack abs pics of Rick???*

And while you in your home office or the den on your laptop scrolling through Rick's pictures you are totally IN YOUR COMPUTER SCREEN. And then your husband sticks his head in and says, "Hi hon...I'm home."

Where in the world did your husband's head come out of nowhere??

Yeah, see, that's the deal with conceal.

Conceal is like a magnet. *You don't want another to know.* So you resist or put out that they better not catch you or see you. See, you are in fact *putting that out.*

That which you resist you get.

Here's a simple example. Take your hand and push it up

against the nearest wall. And keep pushing. You will get more resistance from the wall. Simple.

Now you of course just put this out there and *PING!* in comes your husband's head **ALMOST FINDING OUT** ABOUT YOUR LITTLE ALICE IN WONDERLAND TRIP.

And let me just make a comment about the AFO. Come on boys and girls, surely you know this acronym, right?

The **Almost Found Out.**

Yep. That's a killer. *Your husband didn't find out did he, so what's your worry?*

Because holy-mother-of-mary-he-**almost-found-out** I was looking at Rick. And…(here it comes) *Rick is one of Greg's best friends!*

Crikey.

That's a double barrelled AFO.

Of course Ellen doesn't immediately switch off Rick's personal page. See, women do it with a lot more class. She just looks up from her computer screen and says, "Hi babe, I was just finishing up some Quicken Spreadsheets and I'll get dinner started."

Smooth.

OMG. Men are such Neanderthals. We gotta take some lessons from women. "Quicken Spreadsheets." That's like saying "laundry" to men. They know it needs to be done but they kind of just hear the word "Quicken..." and they're already loosening their tie and getting ready for dinner. I mean what guy is going to go into the den when his wife is just *"finishing up some Quicken Spreadsheets?"*

You might as well have the Black Plague.

Well, Ellen **conceals from sight** her little escapade. She closes up her laptop and still feels guilty. And that's the killer right there.

If you can have "I Dream of Genie" or "I Dream of Jim" *PING!* in on you *anytime anywhere no matter what you are doing, you don't have to conceal a thing.* And you will live a life where you can breathe and not go around with a bunch of AFO's hangin' around your head.

Because in truth, those AFO's never go away. You think they do. But really they are like those little magnets you played with as a kid. These AFO's all just kind of pick up other AFO's that are in the vicinity. Like this:

You go to the kitchen to start dinner and Jim goes to the master bedroom to change into something casual. He hangs up his tie, reaches for his receipts in his back pocket to give to you and notices a receipt near the waste paper basket in your bedroom. He thinks it might be his and doesn't want to not give you all of them as he knows how upset you get if he doesn't. Jim picks up the receipt. It was folded in half. He opens it up and notices it says Nordstrom's at the top.

WARNING: WHOOP WHOOP WHOOP---THE RED

LIGHTS ARE GOING OFF AND THE SIREN IS REALLY LOUD. LIKE AT ONE OF THOSE ATOMIC RADIATION PLANTS WHEN THERE'S A LEAK.

Jim sees "NORDSTROMS" and realizes it's not his. *Whew!*

We're good, right?

Not so fast there Buckaroo.

Jim looks down at what you bought and here is where those tiny little AFO magnets go *clickety-clack-clickety-clack* in the WORLD OF AFO's.

Jim sees the price tag and it registers like this:

THREE HUNDRED AND FIFTY FUCKING BUCKS FOR A FUCKING BLOUSE?

That's what Jim sees. See Jim see. See Jim have smoke coming out of his ears. See Jim almost morph into the Hulk as he walks out to the kitchen.

See Ellen slowing swaying her hips and humming to Andrea Bocelli that is playing softly in the background.

See the trailer for THE WAR OF THE WORLDS II.

Ellen hears her husband coming down the hallway and decides she wants to give him a taste of this *amazing* spaghetti sauce she made and kiss him passionately to get the evening off on a romantic note.

Ummmmm...*Incoming!!!!!!!*

Freeze Frame.

As *a counselor I'm very experienced with handling individuals and couples and* these seemingly magnetic **Almost Found Outs** or **Nearly Found Outs.** In my profession we have a nomenclature that describes this a bit more technically, but I think it clearly makes the point.

Since we're in a Freeze Frame, let's enter the very real world of Ellen:

Here we go...

So Ellen is COMPLETELY in another world right now. NOWHERE NEAR the world that is coming down her hallway like a locomotive about to derail. She has taken her little escapade with Rick and parked it in Alpha Centauri while Andrea Bocelli drowns out any guilt or attention that was there. To help things along she's sipping a little bit of her favorite wine---which is her usual when making spaghetti--- and she is *feelin' fine.* This ambience she is currently in including the wine and aroma of the spaghetti sauce will all play a role in the coming Clash of the Titans Sequel.

And all of this that's coming...*all of it...*is due totally and solely to this investment she and Greg and many us make in the absolute ridiculousness of *hiding. Concealing something from sight* gets sloppy like this receipt. Why? Because concealing something makes you less whole as a being. Remember the white circle and little black dot describing personal integrity from Chapter Two? When you tried to *conceal from sight* the receipt you were not coming from your own integrity. I mean that's just as plain as day, right?

*You are not coming from who you are but **what you have become** which is a partner or spouse that has to hide expensive purchases.*

See this?

And if you take every little tiny microscopic dot as some misstep in your personal integrity, you will begin to see this white circle in a very new light. Just pretend for a moment that there are ten of those tiny baby black magnets floating around there like teenage tadpoles on a Friday night. Your Nordstrom receipt is about ready to magnetize its closest little bad buddy called *"The Hiding of Quicken Spreadsheets."* And once Hulk Husband comes into the kitchen your Nordstrom **Almost Found Out** becomes a **Found Out** and you'll probably spill some of that *amazing* spaghetti sauce on your blouse and stop Bocelli mid note.

And all for what?

To hide the fact that you spent over your budget *but just had to have this blouse.* I mean that's just the simple truth. And what is about to occur doesn't need to occur and you know this.

And you know what the tragic thing is about "stuff" you hide?

It isn't just the emotional toll. It isn't that trust and integrity took a hit. Those are probably the worst fall out. But now, that blouse that you wanted (and is a nice blouse) you may not wear it or if you do it will have to be some time before you go out with your husband in it.

That's why hiding is so ridiculous.

Okay, so we have Ellen about ready to experience *"What is this?"* from her husband as he holds the receipt up in the air and waits for her answer.

Here we go...

Enter Jim.

Jim is incensed. He is about ready to blow a gasket. Jim loves his wife. And he knows she has expensive tastes but this is not the first time he's encountered this with Ellen.

Did somebody say teenage tadpole magnetics?

Jim walks into the kitchen and sees his sexy wife swaying to Bocelli and it smells like heaven. Jim likes Italian. He takes a moment to compose himself. Ummmm...it will take a moment because there literally is steam coming out of his ears.

And true to form, Jim holds up the tiny folded white receipt and looks...no...*announces firmly* to Ellen, *"What is this?"*

Ellen sees her husband is beet red. Not as red as her *amazing* spaghetti sauce. No, like *mad* red. He's holding up a tiny folded piece of paper and asking her *"What is this?"* For a very brief, and I mean *very brief* moment, Ellen is still making love to Jim in her head with Bocelli in the background. That all comes to a screeching halt like in the "old days" when you scraped the turntable arm across the LP.

Ellen *immediately knows* what he's holding. Ellen after all *is* the Receipt Girl don't forget. She's collected those puppies when they've been mangled by her husband but this one...*this one was folded neatly.* A fine, *fine* crease in that receipt. And then Ellen's hand gets weak and she accidently tips that wooden ladle with that *amazing* spaghetti sauce and yep, spills it on her blouse. She sings out to Alexa: "Alexa, stop." and Andrea B's melodic voice ends *abruptly.*

Gulp.

Right. Ellen is experiencing her AFO being revealed. She's having a GM. A *Gulp Moment.*

Ellen knows exactly what this receipt is and her stomach drops like a roller-coaster and her image of lovemaking with her husband dissipates like the IRS were knocking at their door.

She looks at the receipt and looks at her husband.

Not. Good.

Freeze frame.

Okay so how many of you boys and girls have been through something like this? I would imagine we all have.

And where did this all start? Yep. With being online and clicking on a picture or site or something like this and *hiding* it.

Jim hides the tight-butt women yoga videos and Ellen hides her curiosity about handsome Rick and his six pack abs.

I mean just stop and look at that for a minute.

And here's the thing you need to understand and people often miss this: It's not always *the content* of what you are hiding.

IT'S SIMPLY THE FACT THAT YOU ARE HIDING IT.

Women yoga videos are women yoga videos. They do not cause relationship upsets. That's not why those videos are there.

Watching and hiding them like they were porn *creates the air* of an Almost Found Out and an AFO is really truly the soul-breaker.

Because we trust each other. We all know we have aberrations or behavior that aren't always Ozzie and Harriet. We *know* this. That's what makes us human. But when you find out your mate *hid* it, that's **the thing** that takes a little bit of the life force outta you.

Hiding creates distrust.

With the blouse example, even when that gets exposed and talked through, I guarantee neither party will feel like making love tonight. And that's not about price tags or money. That's simply about the soul to soul relationship we each hold so sacred.

These excursions into the rabbit hole of Facebook or online that are hidden always, always, *always* end up with a *Facebreak*. Those tiny little black spot AFO magnets are just that. They hang out just like teenagers with nothing to do. And they can do that for several Friday nights until someone lights up a joint or they get someone to buy them some vodka and then they go out of character and get drunk. And then a parent gets a phone call to come down to the county jail because their wholesome young son stepped over that invisible line and was not so wholesome that night.

It's best that when you enter the rabbit hole that is there in the background of Facebook that you understand, like the teenager example above, that *you don't have to take a whiff of that joint. You don't have to secretly click on a picture of Rick or withhold you are looking at yoga videos.* You don't have to get intoxicated by someone's slick enticing profile pic or be emotionally moved by finding out who your ex is now dating.

You don't have to do that.

You. Just. Don't.

But let's be honest. You are human. And you probably will poke around because curiosity is deeply rooted in all of our DNA as well.

You will "Like" that pic and the pang of "should I or shouldn't I?" will move in and you will say *"it was nothing."*

No, *nothing* is what's left when you hide something from someone you love. Nothing left in your heart. Nothing left in your soul.

And sometimes these breeches go too far for one or both of the parties involved and there's *nothing left to the relationship.*

As Smokey the Bear says, *"Only You Can Prevent Forest Fires."*

DON'T. HIDE. SHIT.

Because only you can prevent that forest fire.

Chapter Eight

Interview with a Stalker

When I set out to write this book, I wanted to know real life experiences from people so I could understand for real, the problems, difficulties, and upset that people were experiencing with Facebook and their relationships.

Honestly, even as long as I've been on Facebook, the survey answers broadened my awareness and brought my understanding to a whole new level.

Facebook wasn't just the most popular online social media site. It was also a place where people were communicating with family and friends and even past relationship partners. It was a place where people admittedly clicked on pictures they liked that resulted in tumult and upset and even relationships being fractured.

Being a certified counselor and consultant I found these revelations by the people who answered the survey humbling and the candidness and honesty in truth lead me to write this book. I want to take a moment here and thank all of the people who took the time to not only answer my surveys and questionnaires, but for your honesty and openness that enabled me to write this book.

One of the surveyees was a young woman. I'll use the pseudo name Catarina27 to protect her real identity. She said she had stalked people on Facebook and other social media sites.

When I initially read this I was like: Holy Crap.

What the hell am I getting into here?

And as a counselor I know this ground well. I understand and respect the revelation from a client about something that they needed me to know. Over forty years of working one-on-one with professional businessmen and couples I have heard the gamut of perversions, affairs, and crossing the invisible line like there's no tomorrow.

And although I had certainly heard of stalking, I had no reason to pay any attention to it. But when Catarina27 answered the survey openly and honestly, I felt an inside look at what an actual stalker does would be illuminating and helpful.

Helpful?

Yes. Because we all to a certain degree like to believe "I would never do that" like it's the gospel truth. We all justify these kinds of things. "It's not stalking. I need to know what my ex is doing."

The fact is you become free the moment that you are honest with yourself and admit that yes, *"I guess now that I look at it I did a bit of stalking of my ex-husband."*

The point of this book has not been to moralize or slap your hand or put down some new code. That's for you to work out. The purpose of this book was to illuminate occurs every day with regular people like you and I and that yes, the Rabbit Hole can be enticing, fun, and intoxicating, but too much booze can also land you in the slammer.

I have to say I admire the courage of Catarina27. She doesn't pull any punches. She answered the interview questions honestly, and if you read her answers without prejudice, I think you will see she is a young girl who does have a moral compass. Her interview was enlightening and brought to view scenarios that will help me as I counsel and consult couples moving forward.

And yes, I hope it is enlightening and helpful to you.

Here is the interview in full:

Do you recall the very first time you stalked someone on Facebook?

Yes.

Me: Did you know prior to going ahead with stalking this person that you were in fact stalking them or did you somehow "color" this activity with some other description?

Catarina27: Yes, but of course I considered it "research".

Me: Just curious, the whole concept of stalking involves pursuing someone stealthy---unseen and hidden. Did this give you some kind of "rush" or adrenaline high knowing you were in fact spying on this person?

Catarina27: Heck yeah!

Me: When you first started stalking, what did you find most exciting about it?

Catarina27: Getting to know the inner secrets of my "stalkee". Learning many aspects of my target that they would not know that I know so that I can (when we meet someday) talk about similar interests as if, oh my gosh, we have SO much in common!!!! Ok, all joking aside, it is important to me to learn as much as possible about a person that I'm interested in to see if there are any glaring outpoints BEFORE I invest my time. I really want to "vet" the person before I decide to take it further, say, like talk on the phone or, oh-my-gosh, go on a date!

Me: Was there a downside to stalking, i.e. did you come across things you wish you hadn't found out---like you had gone too far but there was no turning back?

Catarina27: Well, I have done this as an employer and discovered a mug shot and was very glad I did my "research" before continuing any further.

When it comes to stalking potential lovers, I have never found any information - no matter how bad!!! - that made me wish I hadn't found out. Even the WORST of details truly only makes me feel a deeper sense of understanding of that person.

Me: Approximately how many times have you stalked different people?

Are you kidding? Do you think I could count that? Dozens and dozens. And dozens. I stalk men and women. I want to see who are the friends of this "person of interest". How "friendly" is this man with these other women?

Me: At any time did that person suspect you were stalking them or "was there ever a close call?"

Well, if I stalked someone and then we did actually meet and strike up a friendship, we would discuss the mutual stalking aspect of our activities with humor. But that is only IF the meeting became successful and developed into "sharing our secrets" with each other. The more intense the activity of stalking only betrayed that the interest was more intense. It truly is the ultimate in compliments.

I never had a close call that I know of.

With LinkedIn you can see who has recently viewed your profile, which is a way of being discovered. But you can still view a person's profile on LinkedIn without logging in, which doesn't make your "View" visible to the person. ;)

I also do my stalking in "incognito" mode on google. (Ctrl-Shift-N) That way, if anyone breaks into my computer, they have no proof that I've been stalking.

Besides that, I'm not so sure how one could be busted at it.

I did have a case of "friend requesting" one love interest's female friends. In this case, there was one female friend that was pretty obscure (like we had no mutual friends other than this man) -- that was dangerous. But I openly admitted (with humor) that I had done so. Truthfully, I think it only endeared me more to my new man...he saw that I was kinda freakishly "into" him, in a "not-quite-too-scary fiercely and intensely interested in him" way. He kinda dug it. :)

Me: Have you had people call you on it, meaning that they challenged you or sent you a query as to their feeling they were being stalked?

Catarina27: Interestingly, I had a boyfriend ask me one time if I was stalking him, and he was truly disappointed when the answer was no.

Any other times someone challenged me of stalking, it was from a boyfriend love interest and when the answer was yes, this was only taken as a complete turn-on.

Me: Like a burglar that gets past the best security, give us an example of what exactly you do to stalk a person. Give us an inside look.

Catarina27: Oooooohhhhhh......you REALLY want to know???????
You can stalk better with some phone apps than online with a pc...such as: Instagram which was developed as a phone app....you can see who has "liked" an instagram photo ONLY while using the phone app....not while using your pc. Fun stalker fact, huh?

I go to the person's FaceBook page, look at their timeline first. What do they find important to post about? How amazing their sports team is? How amazing their abs are? How important politics are in their life? What kind of pictures do they post? Are they classy or trashy? Diplomatic or inflammatory? Superficial or intellectual? Sensitive or crude? Focused on themselves, or interested in others? If it's within range of acceptability - i.e., not TOO freakishly devoted to any one activity or interest - be it sports, watching tv, partying, drinking or taking selfies...I usually make mental note but continue...

Then I look at their "About" section. Where did they grow up? Where did they go to school? How well-educated are they? What was their major if they went to college? What is their birthday? Then I take a quick detour to research our love signs and make sure that we are an acceptable match. If the horoscopes are too far out of alignment, it's all over at that point.

All joking aside...back to the about section. How old are they? If they don't post their birth year, you can still tell by the year they graduated from high school, college, etc. Are they WAAAY to old or WAAAAY too young? If not, safe to continue. (Well, even if they're waaaay too young, I pretty much continue....)

How do they describe their politics? Their religion? I usually -- no matter what their answer may be -- like to know. If they state their political stance or their religion without being vague - I like that! It shows they're strong and comfortable with who they are. If they state it with diplomacy and more generality - I like that too! It shows they care about getting along with others, with creating agreement rather than differences. This stalking part for me is all about getting to know that person, how they choose to describe themselves, how they communicate. Are they an extremist in any way? If not, safe to continue.

Then I look at all of their photos: Photos of them (that they've been tagged in), photos that they've posted, and any and all albums they've created. This gives an intimate look into their past, their friends (too many party pictures?) and oh, the juicy part: their past loves and relationships. I like to see that. Were they married? Dated a lot? How did they look in those pictures? Happy and in love? I like to see that! An excess of current pics with pretty women who are not relatives? If not, safe to continue.

Then I head back to their timeline. I scroll down and click on every picture, watch every video. This tells me about what they find important, and what they want to communicate and share with others. Tells a lot about them. Then I look at every single person who liked each and every post. If there is a flurry of "likes and comments" around one particular time frame, especially with comments such as "Oh Joe, that's hilarious!!!!!!" well then I know for SURE they fucked. I look to see if that person is still actively liking and commenting in present time. If not, they're not currently fucking, so...safe to continue.

Come on, this is basic stalking 101, right?

Then I go to my own search bar and type that person's name and find any other pictures, pages or posts that person has made. I find whose timelines they've written on, what pretty girl friend pics they liked, and what they posted on other people's pages. Too many likes and comments on other pretty girl pictures? If not, safe to continue.

I then look at their friends list and look at each friend's page (if it poses a threat - as in, pretty single lady of possible competition). I make mental note. I look at that person's page and postings and scroll down their timeline to see if my man has "liked" or "commented" on too many of their pics, especially profile pics or pretty selfies. If not, safe to continue.

The stalking may continue then outside of Facebook. Oh, who am I kidding? Of COURSE it does! Google that person's name, name with middle initials, full name, towns they lived in, places they've worked, positions they've held, groups they belonged to, any other public pictures or information, women they were married to, places they lived, places they currently live, see if they own or rent, how much their mortgage was, complete with Google Satellite so you can peek in on them right now, see what kind of car they drive, see if they are sharing their abode with anyone else....all of these things can be helpful in the risk-o-meter. Is this person worthwhile investing in emotionally or not? Is this person worth a text back and forth of "hey...", or not? Is this person worth the next big step of deciding: should you pick up the phone if they call?

And most of all, with all of this depth of information...should you say yes if they ask you out on a date?

Me: When you stalked someone, did you find out data that was actually important for you to know for your own good or for the welfare of another? And if so, could you share with us what that was?

Catarina27: Yes, when I was in HR at a company and found a mug shot of a current job applicant. That was awesome!!!!

Now romantically, I also was stalking and found a mug shot. I have to tell you the truth: it only endeared me more to my "stalkee". Would I date him? Well, deep down, there's a wild side of me that would love to. In reality, probably not. (Because I KNOW my father is ALSO STALKING each and every one of my boyfriends with just as much fervor!) But I think -- nay, I know -- I love him even more because of that mug shot. It showed that he was a "real" person, with his own struggles. I knew him enough in my current life to know that he had overcome that dark past, and it made me admire him more for that. And it kinda turned me on. BTW, that secret I would have only kept to myself if not for this interview.

Me: Have you ever been caught?

Catarina27: Yes! I admitted it! Once I confessed, the whole dirty truth spilled out.....all the details, the ways I stalked him, how I researched every. single. woman that was his friend, how I poured over their pages, their pictures, seeing how many times my man "liked" their pictures or made a comment, and if so, what was the comment...all of it.

But the confessions were done with humor, without judgment, and in fact, with admiration from the "stalkee" regarding the extent to which I invested to find out AS MUCH AS POSSIBLE about this man. In his eyes, it was completely flattering -- the ultimate of compliments.

And that admission -- and the welcoming way in which it was accepted -- also opened the door to talking in detail about both of our pasts: our mistakes, our past loves, what went wrong with them, etc. It was a beautiful catalyst to exploring the most intimate depths of each other.

Me: Although stalking carries with it a bad connotation, have you found instances where stalking was beneficial? Can you share an experience in this regard?

When I told my lover I had stalked him, it made him feel like I really cared and was interested in him. He loved hearing about it! It fed his ego. It was awesome to share with him; he knew I was being honest with him, admitting my flaws with him, telling him my secrets, showing my vulnerabilities.

Now, on the downside, when I was going through troubles in a relationship, this subject of stalking brought out the WORST. My ex admitted to me that he stayed up late, already in the worst of moods, then on top of that exhausted, seeing all the men liking my current posts on Facebook and just getting more and more upset. He would look at the men, judge how attractive they were, if they were single and (worst of all) living in the same town, then it went from bad to worse down the spiral of despair. It made him feel that I was purposefully making posts to promote myself and to seek "likes" from men. This made him so upset that he decided to "unfriend" and even block me to stay away from the torture caused by seeing my postings and the subsequent "likes", feeding his worst imagination of the relationships I was developing with these other men. His stalking became very destructive to my attempts to remain friends after the break up.

The same has occurred for me: if I feel vulnerable in a relationship, and if I then turn to stalking to gain insight into this person I'm feeling vulnerable with, it usually turns bad for me. I see the pretty girls they're friends with, and not knowing any details, my imagination puts the "worst" scenario there. It just makes me start to feel worse and more insecure. I'm wise enough to this though that I just STOP when I find this happening and unplug. And I make sure that I don't feel too badly that my abs aren't as good as the other pretty girls, or that I didn't go skiing in the Alps last week like Susan did. I get to work on myself and creating my own life to be worthwhile, industrious, rewarding, and of value to others. And try to post as many pics about it on facebook as possible. (Just kidding.)

Me: Do you still stalk today?

Catarina27: I will always be a stalker.

It is in my nature to know as much as possible about others, about their lives, about their friends, about their likes and dislikes, about their aspirations and what they thrive on. I want to know those things as much as possible. Social media such as Facebook feeds this passion.

I know the primary risk of stalking to me is the instilling of a sense of inferiority. If I see my love interest (or worse, the beautiful single women who are his friends) doing something interesting or helpful for others, creating their lives in a beautiful way -- without me -- there can be a little "twinge" that makes me feel badly. Then, as the "likes" from the single, beautiful girls (and oh yes, I stalk each and every one of them to make sure how single, how beautiful, and just how accessible they are) pour in, I descend down into the hell of feeding the worst demons of my imagination. I do my best to just STOP my activity at that point and turn OFF the electronic device. I then invest in myself by going to bed (it's usually late at night that I get into that kind of destructive activity) and turning my thoughts to actions I can take to improve my value to myself and others.

But I will never stop stalking. I cherish any and every insight into a person's soul, into the parts of them they would not think or dare to tell me but which is an innate part of what makes them unique. It fills in the detail and provides a deeper understanding of them with all the subtle harmonics, the highlights and the shadows.

I KNOW that there is NO substitute for getting to know a person face to face. I KNOW that I should not prejudge a person and I honestly seek to reserve my judgment and give most men the benefit of the doubt. I know that what I read online is not always true. I know that what I read online is sometimes one-sided and is spurned from jealousy or greed or vested interests. I know that one's past is NOT to be held against a person. I judge a person by who they are in the present. In fact, I usually find a troubled past only all the more endearing - I can have compassion for their struggles and their battle wounds. So long as I can see that they are sincere now and working to become better - that is what matters to me: who is this person in front of me, today? Any flaws I find only makes that person so much more "real" to me. I only use this "research" to fill in the colors of the beautiful picture of the person that is appearing before me.

And nothing beats the life that is in that person today.

Usually, in the end, after all that time spent stalking, I determine I'd better just get to know that person by talking with them and meeting with them and finding out simply who this person is today.

Perhaps we just might get along.

Thanks very much for this interview and being so candid.

Chapter Nine

What You See Is Not Always What You Get

In probably one of the most emotional survey questions I posed, individuals and couples answered that there were some real *Facebreaks* when they met the person in real life and they were not entirely like the picture they had on Facebook or online.

This brings to light this whole idea of the digital or online world vs. the real world. With the advance of technology many of the pictures taken are HD quality, leaving one to believe *"Wow, she looks great for being 50!"* or *"Damn look at those abs!"*

Hold your horses, there partner.

Did you know that they had Adobe Photoshop in the Wild Wild West?

I have to be perfectly honest, when I did my research on what I cover in this chapter, I wasn't aware of the *extent* to which both men and women edit or touch-up their photos.

I know I have some old school DNA running through my veins, but I missed that train to No Blemish City. And I even missed the next train that said it was headed to the city of Photo Shop My Abs.

So while I waited for my train, I Googled **"editing selfies on Facebook"** and came up with:

7,510,000 search results.

Okay campers, that's: SEVEN MILLION FIVE HUNDRED TEN THOUSAND.

And here's just one excerpt from an article I read:

"Nearly three-quarters (70%) of Gen Y/Millennial women edit their pictures before posting them to their social networks, but so do more than half of men surveyed in the same age group (18-34). What's more, nearly 60% of parents with children under 18 edit their pictures before posting them on social networks. Even among respondents ages 55 – 64, more than a third (32%) are editing their self-images."

And here's just another random headline:

68 Percent of Adults Edit Their Selfies Before Sharing Them With Anyone

Me: *"Houston, we are leaving the moon orbit. We are igniting the re-entry thrusters into Earth's atmosphere. We will be hitting the Van Allen Belts and then the Sixty Eight Percent Photo Editing Belt. Our onboard computers tell us that because there has been so much editing we may miss our splashdown site. We do not want to land in the Himalayas, Houston. Do you copy? Over"*

Houston: *"Copy that Apollo 17. NASA Computers indicate someone hacked your landing site coordinates and has photoshopped you landing in a whore house in Nevada. We are correcting that now. We will get you home Apollo 17. You might want to take a selfie of you and your crew before you hit that band and be sure you edit out any signs of perspiration or stress. You gotta look good for the press when you splash down. Over"*

Me: *"Houston, we need to come down in water. Repeat, we need to come down in water. The Pacific Ocean. And not my Aunt's bathtub in Iowa. Do you copy, Houston? Over"*

Houston: *"Copy that, Apollo 17. Just look good when you land. Over."*

We long ago moved out of sharing pictures like Polaroids and Kodak that were all spontaneous. We've morphed into mini-versions of Warner Bros or Paramount Studios. We even have our own make-over apps too.

I'm. Not. Kidding.

As the fictional TV character Gomer Pyle would say with his high tenor voice from Mayberry, North Carolina:

"Surprise, Surprise, Surprise."

Enter **Perfect365:**

"One free app, **Perfect365,** calls itself a "one-tap makeover" and allows people to quickly smooth out their skin, eradicating pores and covering up spots. Users of the app can also opt for a more radical makeover, allowing them to try out new makeup looks in bright colours.

But people are not using the app to try out new eyeshadow combinations - a whopping **80 per cent** of its users opt for the "natural" setting which blurs imperfections and evens out skin tone.

I can just *feel* all the people who have stopped reading this page right now and are switching over to their iPhone or Android and typing *Perfect365* as friggin' fast as they can.

And this excerpt below is a *real world example* of a girl writing her experience of editing her picture and her boyfriend's reaction:

"Earlier this summer I took a selfie on the beach. After I adjusted the photo and prepared to publish it on Instagram, my boyfriend said, "That doesn't even look like you, Levi." I argued that I only added a filter, which might have been a bit of a stretch. So I smudged all my wrinkles, changed my eye color, and plumped up my lips. Big deal! It's just a selfie, right? (fstoppers.com 2016)

I have to be honest here. When I posed this survey on Facebook the answers I got back were the first layer of this crazy maze. And some of you reading this might be like, *"Nothing new here, we've been editing and touching up our selfies since we got our first zit."*

Well, this whole idea of edited or fake pics pushed me to look further into the actual background of Facebook. If you are a Facebook fanatic you will know it has a fairly storied background. It's like some a whole season of Boston Legal gone crazy. For those of you that don't know this fun fact, Facebook's original name was Facemash. That's right. Facemash.

And what was the original purpose of Facemash?

"The website was set up as a type of <u>"hot or not" game</u> for Harvard students. The website allowed visitors to compare two student pictures side-by-side and let them decide who was hot or not." (Wikipedia.com)

So here is Mark Zuckerberg as a college student at Harvard back in 2003, comparing two student pictures side-by-side and deciding *"who was hot or not."*

So when you click on Cindy's picture to check out her hot bod or Michael's picture to check out his abs it's like walking across an old Indian burial site on Facebook. The *ghosts of checking out pics and that mysterious invisible line* are in the very fabric of what this site was built on.

I wasn't kidding about the Wild Wild West!

So, this all lead me to bring to light what we all have encountered at one time or another, and that is:

WHAT IS REPRESENTED ON THE OUTSIDE VS. WHAT IS ACTUALLY UNDERNEATH.

Just for fun, let's take apart the word "Facebook." Since Facebook's origins began with pictures of *"who's hot and who's not"* which at is about the *outside or surface*, stay with me here and see its meaning both as a noun and a verb. Don't worry. I'm not going to "go all grammar police" on you here. But I think you'll find this interesting.

Face:

noun
1. the front part of a person's head from the forehead to the chin.
2. the surface of a thing, especially one that is presented to view.

verb
1. confront and deal with or accept.

Okay, so on the outside and very visible in most every Facebook profile is the picture of the person's *face.* And remember this is a *picture* of their face. This is not their *actual* face. I know, you may have to read that again. It is a picture. And it is most likely edited.
And if you think your friend's pic who you've known all your life looks just like that, don't be writing me later that they in fact *did have zits.* Sheriff Dave warned you!

Let's start with men looking at and clicking on pictures of women:

Survey results showed men were not happy campers at all when the woman they met in real life did not look like the pictures they had clicked on on Facebook.

Many of the pictures were of the women being younger. Unless they had a hot bod, the body shots were few or none because hello... no woman in their right mind is going to post a body pic if they are self-conscious about their figure or weight or both.

Well, this is the *noun* definition of *face*. The thing is that in today's society you truly do have *two faces*. You have the *edited selfie face*, and then how *your mug appears* when you finally meet at Starbucks.

Bill: (Looking around for a 5' 6" blonde. Bill sees who *he thinks* is Cindy). *"Hi, are you Cindy?"*
Cindy: (Cindy turns around and she has her *first Facebreak*). *"Oh ahhh*...(smiling/shocked/feeling-like-she-made-a-mistake) Hi... are you Bill?"
Bill: (Holy crap. She's taller than me. And she's heavier than her picture). *"Yes, I'm Bill. Can I buy you a cup of coffee?"*
Cindy. (Shit! He's older than what his picture showed. His hair is thinning too. And his teeth...) *"Yes, yes...that would be great."*

FACEBREAK!!!

Hear the air raid sirens?

Now this obviously is not indicative of how all encounters go but truly there are many more like this that happen every day and the biggest problem is NOT that these two people are not compatible. They may end up dating. They may become great friends.

The point here is that there was a meeting of *two different worlds.*

Facebook Cindy: *"Hello Bill, meet my real world weight."*
Facebook Bill: *"Hello Cindy, meet my real world hair... or lack of it, anyway."*

All of us to some degree have been wooed and romanced and *"Hollywooded"* to the nth degree so that in this culture now, when the digital person we "met" online comes into the real world, all of our digital virtual fantasies of this other person start falling out of the sky like some overzealous hunter shooting doves on the first day of hunting season.

What Bill and Cindy are in fact experiencing *right at this moment* as Bill walks with her over to order coffees, is what I refer to as the:

BEWILDERMENT INSTANT.

Both Bill and Cindy are bewildered as to *"how in the hell did I miss that he/she was not what I saw from the pictures online?"*

Talk about *awkward.*

But this *is* the person. Like we learned in school. The definition of a noun. A person, place, or thing. Well, here's the *real person* in *a real place.*

Reminds me years ago when the movie "An Interview with a Vampire" came out and Brad Pitt was cast. People were like WTF? Brad Pitt as a Vampire?? See? Many had their own ideas about who or what Brad Pitt represented in their minds. They could not reconcile their idea of Brad Pitt with having him be a vampire. Celluloid Break. Just made that up. I can do that because this is the Age of Friggin' Acronyms.

Okay, so we'll leave Bill and Cindy to work out their fate. And to be fair there are plenty of stories of people meeting and becoming good friends and some ending up even getting married.

But this chapter is about **What You See is Not Always What you Get** so let's return to the flip side of this.

Mary clicks on pictures of Ed on Facebook. She clicks on his picture and he looks pretty handsome. There are a few other pics but not too many. Mary is not really into how the man looks physically as much as she is really into wanting him to have a great personality, etc. She admits they cannot be ugly, but *she says she doesn't put a lot of attention on just the guys physical appearance.*

Mary meets Ed and finds out Ed *is actually balding.* Not like anything in his picture. (True Story)

Freeze Frame.

Okay, I don't know who you are Mr. Ed, but you're so not representin' the species doing that kind of shit, you know what I mean?

This gives us dudes a bad rep online. Very bad. It's bad enough guys are spraying their abs to glisten when they take selfies. It's craaaaazeee that some of you guys think the whole "holding your belly in" works when you take a pic. I mean are you going to wear a friggin' girdle when you meet a girl? And stop with the whole *"Can't you seem I'm ripped?"* pics. I've never known a woman to put BIG BICEPS at the top of her list of things she's looking for in a relationship or marriage. Unless maybe if you'd help carry the laundry with those big guns. *You do laundry, Ed?*

Okay. End of rant. But *seriously?*

So this brings us to the second definition of face as a noun which is *"the surface of a thing, especially one that is presented to view."*

That's right. The *surface* of a thing. And this is important to remember. Facebook is all digital. It is all pixels and things like those freaky fluorescent green dots of code from the Matrix under the surface. You have editing tools so that pictures remove blemishes and heighten one's tan, etc. And believe me these things are all done to make that *surface* look better. Same reason you clean your house before company comes over. The surface of things has got to be more presentable.

But the irony is when we switch to the *verb* form of Face we find this:

verb
1. confront and deal with or accept.

See when we have to confront someone in real life then we move into *the ability to confront, deal with, or accept.*

Many of the couples who answered the surveys answered because they were in truth having a hard time *confronting, dealing with, and accepting* that their partner did something that they in fact could not confront or minimally was hard to experience.

So we go from the *noun* of Face which really is just *the surface of things* to the *verb* or action form of Face which is really what this entire book brought to light.

When you look at six pack abs, pretty girls, Lamborghinis, houses in Bali or whatever, *you are in fact looking at the surface of things.*

But *clicking* and *liking* are verbs in motion. That is now moving into *doing* something that may then be hard for another *to deal with or accept.*

Facebook can be a lot of things. It can be a place to see your kids across the state or videos of your grandkids. You can watch YouTube videos of a Coldplay concert or just stop and have your heart melt watching the cutest video of husky puppies that you've ever seen. *It's all of that.*

And much, much more.

And part of that "much, much more" can be the parts that are *underneath* the surface. The cat videos and posed happy couple pictures can be a bit like the mint on the pillow at your stay in the Hilton Hotel. It's really nice. But it's still a mint. And it's there to create an effect. And if you've come back from dinner having had a *Facebreak* with your partner all the mints in the world don't change that. And what you were arguing at over dinner was in fact *what was underneath the surface.*

One woman in the survey made mentioned that she was just really bothered by a picture her husband shared of her *without asking her*. It *embarrassed* her. It caused a *Facebreak*. For *real*. And she was beside herself. Do you know why?

She was shocked that he didn't have the courtesy to just ask her if it was okay with her to post.

Simple, huh?

But this is the stuff of *Facebreaks*. This is where *confronting* and *dealing* with these actions becomes hard for both sides. For all the jealousies that occur because of actions *known about* by one another on the surface, there is no greater tragedy than what is occurring underneath the surface.

Underneath the Surface and Who We Are:

During the time I was researching Facebook and online behavior a friend of mine related a story to me that I think highlights the above and more of what I want to summarize below.

Let's call My friend Joe. Joe told me about another good friend of mine, a very prominent, successful, and wealthy businessman. Let's call him Richard. He's well known and could be considered by many to be a celebrity. He is on Facebook and other social media platforms. He and his wife are very visible online.

Joe related to me that he lived next door to this celebrity in an upscale gated condo community. He said he hardly ever sees him, even though he lives next door. Joe went on to tell me that one night he heard Richard and his wife screaming and yelling so loud you could *feel* it through the walls. He said it was like crazy banshee screaming.

Yep. Real world. Shit.

You will *never* see *that* on Facebook. *You never see any of what's below the surface.* And part of Joe's narrative about this incident was that this was the first time he'd heard them argue like that *and it didn't match up with what he knew from seeing him online.* You could tell while he was relating this that it wasn't *just* the yelling. It was the *difference between his digital or virtual reality of this person and the real world experience.* I could *see* Joe's Supercomputer mind trying to add it all up.

Your mind can't add what's not there.

There are *missing* happy face pixels. There are missing Cancun tans and million dollar smiles. The whole *"I wish I could be like them feelings"* are *missing.* The mind is just *whirrrrrrrrring.* It's trying to compute. It's trying to add it up. These are the same people posing in front of their Mercedes looking larger than life.
The mind cannot get the right answer as data has been edited out. Your mind will jam. It will come to a halt. Joe's Supercomputer whirrrs but he's not getting any print-out. So he's gotta talk about it.

Because he's trying to reconcile his Facebook World with the Real World.

Ain't. Gonna. Reconcile.

In truth Joe's Facebook experience of Dick and Jane is simply the *noun* relationship. It's the professional headshot picture. It's the glossy book cover and the posed beach photos that make you wish you had what they have.

Well it's completely okay to wish for that if that's what you want.

But don't ever forget that's the *noun* version you're looking at.

It's a person, place, or thing on Facebook. A digital, virtual world.

And on Facebook except for candid or goofy photos most of the pictures as noted earlier in this chapter are edited and posed. Posed People. Beach places. Shiny cars and boats.

I've handled plenty of arguments with couples but I can tell you for 100% sure *none* of those yelling matches were *posed.*

And if Joe went next door and just opened the front door and just walked right in unannounced on Dick and Jane he would be confronting the *verb* form of that relationship. He would *not* see the million dollar smiles. He would have thought he walked through the wrong door. He would have thought he entered Bizarro World or for sure he had *the wrong couple.* Because these two, were not the warm and fuzzy Colgate Smile Couple he knew from Facebook.

And I will tell you from 40 years of working with individuals and couples, that what Joe just walked in on is in truth *quite a lot to confront and deal with* if you are not trained. The cartoons that show a spouse throwing a frying pan come from real life. The cartoonist is adding some comic relief with the unbelievability of the guy getting hit with a frying pan.

However, when you see a woman who's just had a crazy argument with her husband nursing her black eye with an ice pack, the comic relief comes to a screeching halt.

Chapter Ten

Make No Mistake. That Pic is Probably Fake.

I felt this subject needed a chapter to itself. This is the whole look at the underbelly of what is fake or false on Facebook or online.

Even today, for the first time in my lifetime we have this idea of "Fake News" in our headlines. This idea of *fake* is morphing like the plague in our society.

So in my research I got right to it. I Googled "posting fake pics on Facebook" and I got this:

8,220,000 searches. 8 *m-i-l-l-i-o-n.*

Okay, to some of you this isn't new news. For those of us who are a tad late to this party and in the spirit of this book and I feel it's important to shed some light on this subject of what do we mean by *fake?* In doing my research it turned my head. And that's a good think you know?

It was like a wake up call because you think when you read about "fake profiles" that that's a bunch of whacked out Internet trolls who are sitting in their rooms late at night eating Cheetos amped up on Red Bull killing time making fake Facebook profiles *just to fuck you up.*

Well I can assure you those boys and girls are doing that for sure.

And that's not the scariest part. See you'd kind of expect that, right?

But when you find you look over your own friends and you confront that Steve or Kathy do not look like that in real life, not *really,* you kind of feel like scrolling off their picture because *something about their picture doesn't sit right with you.*

That's right.

*It doesn't sit right with you because there **is** something **not** right.*

And it makes you feel just a tad uneasy. Like hearing your best friend tell a lie to another friend of yours right in front of you. The white lie came out smooth as silk and it was so white you almost didn't detect it. But when it came out you actually could feel the lie in your own soul. You're like: OMG. Brian just lied to Virginia about what we doing last night. You nervously laugh and go on.

Yeah. It doesn't feel right because it's *false.*

White lie. Green lie. Rainbow colored lie. Doesn't matter. IT'S A LIE. And I mentioned this in an earlier chapter but it bears repeating here; I firmly believe that no matter where we all came from that when we took the turn-off for Earth, we all have this innate sense of *what is true.* And throughout our collective experiences we've been lied to so many times that we may not know which way is up sometimes. But when we see or detect something that is *not* genuine, our "Truth o'

Meter" goes off. And we may not know *what* to do, but we know something is giving us this queasy feeling. We all know what it's like to tell the white lie like Bryan and also be witness to another who tells the white lie in your presence. It's just fucks with our inherent Truth Strand of DNA.

Kathy's pic? That's a headshot from four years ago. Nice shot. But she does *not* look like that now. And Steve's pic? Geezus. You know Steve drinks. You just saw him at the grocery store and the drinking has taken a toll on that once handsome face of his.

And then lets go down deeper into this Rabbit Hole and see how in the hell you have a fake friend?

Jill: *"Hi..Bryan...I'm Jill."*
Bryan: *"Ah...Hi Jill...do we know each other?"*
Jill: (feigning surprise). *"Yes, we're friends on Facebook!"*

Freeze frame.

Now boys and girls this is happens all the time out there in the Wild Wild West. I know some of you have experienced something similar.

So here's a Pop Quiz for you:

What do you think Bryan does now?

Well, to tell you the truth Bryan is caught in the real world nebulae. And to be fair, if the roles were reversed and this was Jill, they'd both be in momentarily suspended in the

BEWILDERMENT INSTANT we discussed in Chapter Seven.

And let's clarify that instant a tad more here:

It's that infinitesimally teeny-tiny moment that the virtual world meets the real world all at once with NO PATTERN RECOGNITION.

Bryan puts his eye up to the Security Camera Platform ala Mission Impossible to get through to the other side and the RED LIGHT IS GOING OFF.

Bryan is BEWILDERED. He is SUPPOSED TO KNOW Jill. His Supercomputer mind is burning up fuses like an FBI computer matching the police's sketch of the murder suspect. Millions upon millions of pictures are flashing through Bryan's mind to get a MATCH.

Women with jet black hair whiz by. Smiles. Big blue eyes. Green eyes. Brown eyes. Boob pics. Bikini pics. Cocktail dress pics. Everything in an INSTANT is seeking a match. Another red light is flashing.

WARNING: NO MATCH FOUND. WE DO NOT RECOGNIZE THIS PERSON. PROCEED WITH CAUTION.

So Bryan is meeting Jill and she is right in front of him. She said they were friends and Bryan, in this slow-motion split second realizes he sometimes does "friend" girls just because they are pretty. And well, Jill is pretty and well, he doesn't want to be rude, so….

See what Bryan does?

Bryan has a no match. But he doesn't want to be rude. So here's the kicker and some of you might disagree with this but that's okay this is not Law and Order here. This is a comment on the behavior people go through.

Bryan now has to actually be somewhat fake or false himself.

So Bryan will have to pretend a bit because he did apparently "Like" her picture. But is Bryan being himself? Not entirely. And he's not pendulum swinging to the far side of fake which would be:

"Ohhhhh..yessss! Of course, *now* I remember you! Just took me a minute! How are you?"

Ugh.

That's totally fake and false and the Security Guards are coming over and hauling Bryan's ass out of the building.

Now I know what you're thinking: "Dave, this is not true for me. All my friends on Facebook are real." You are obviously talking about some of these really crazy people on Facebook, not me."

Okee dokee. Let's just get a real simple definition of fake here:

Fake:

Noun: anything made to appear otherwise than it actually is; counterfeit.

Verb: to conceal the defects of or make appear more attractive, interesting, valuable, etc., usually in order to deceive.

Alright, "*So Mrs. I Have Only Real Friends, would you mind looking over these mug shots of your 317 friends with the detective and see if any of them look like they **appear otherwise than they actually are** or **are concealing defects or making themselves more attractive?***"

"*It's okay, take your time...I'll wait....*"

Listen. I had a wake-up call myself researching and writing this chapter. I'm just being honest here. I realized I have two very good friends on Facebook who are using pictures of themselves which are at least eight to ten years ago. I know one for sure because she used that same picture on a dating site eight years ago. And you know what your mind does? It begins to rationalize it's *not* fake. See, it's not *really* fake. Not *my* friends. See? You will give your friends the benefit of doubt. "So what if her profile pic is from 10 years ago." "That's just Kathy." It's just a bunch of bullshit rationalization.

The thing is there is probably no one on this planet that likes this word *fake*. Fake eyelashes. Fake boobs. Fake hairpiece. Fake smile.

And let me be clear here: It's not that fake is bad. Good and bad are simply one's own viewpoint or consideration about things. I think fake eyelashes are weird. So what?

It's the fact that you need to up your Spidey Sense when you see false or fake. See? If your girlfriend tells you Steve the Drinker asked her out on a date after a night of texting back and forth and she said,

"Whaddya think, Jill?

Well what *do* you think, Jill? Hmmm?

Are you going to tell her be ready for ruddy-faced Steve because he tends to spend too many nights with his friend Jim Beam?

Or are you going to nervously say, *"Wow, that's so great Cathy, I'm so happy for you!"* and then toss and turn all night because Cathy is one of your best friends and well...she should know...*shouldn't she?*

Jill?

See this whole idea of false or fake has gone way *way* beyond the borders of good or bad. You have now entered the world of *what is real* regarding your friend Cathy and her excitement with her text convo with Steve.

This has *nothing* to do with what is good or bad. *Nothing.*

It's simply: *do **you** know what's true or not?* See because it goes back to our own Truth o' Meter. If we're told that Steve dyes his hair we know it up front. It *looked* like it didn't it? I mean he *tells* you. That counts for *something,* right? At least he's not being false about it. It's just weird sitting at dinner knowing he does and you just *have to know the truth.* And when you know you are no longer trapped by the not-know of it.

Okay, well, if we're all trying to *confront, deal with, and accept,* shouldn't the first step be, *being honest with ourselves?*

Tell me if you have any pictures in your 317 friends that are **concealing defects or making themselves more attractive?**

If you lie to me I'm calling Perry Mason. Swear. To. God.

Okay, you discover you have some "fake" friends!

Freeze Frame.

"Dave, they're really not fake. Fake is if they…."

"Dave, it's really just semantics here...my friend Sally has gained weight since her divorce and she just hasn't changed her picture…"

Ummm…okaaaayy. Can you send a Smoke Signal or put up a Facebook Ad alerting Joe and Bill and all those cowboys that hope to meet your friend Sally that's online before they start fantasizing some kind of Shades of Grey elevator scene with her?

See? *Facebreak.*

And if you think I'm slicing this baloney a bit thin I ask you to just step back and confront what exactly is going on, online.

We have all been lulled to sleep by cosmetics and movies and appearance. And we've been so intoxicated by it we have in many cases lost our senses and have actual real world upsets *because the picture of the guy or girl did not add up to who we saw online.*

There is no slicing this baloney too thin if it wakes people up to the fact that our worlds have been morphing over several decades to where upwards of 70% of the people who upload pictures on the largest social media site in the world are editing those pics to **conceal defects** or **make themselves more attractive.**

Is it the end of the world? Of course not. Not even close.

But I will tell you when I have talked to people who have experienced these real life *Facebreaks,* you could tell from their voices and emotion that they **_felt_** like their world was caving in on them.

And why?

Because all of us, since we were knee high to a grasshopper, believed in the *realness* of life. We knew sharing our peanut butter jelly sandwich with Billy *was what it was.* When he shared *his* cheese sandwich it was *real.* When we skinned our knees on the playground it was *real.* Sally had freckles. That *was* Sally. It's why we liked Sally. She didn't photoshop them out. And Billy had a birthmark on his neck so we asked our Mom what it was and we were cool with that.

Life. Was. Real.

And since it was real we *trusted i*t. There was no reason *not* to trust it. Joey had an Italian accent and we thought he was just the best because he sounded different and *that too* was cool. And when Mary came to school with pigtails and yellow ribbons we were like amazed.

Mary was killin' it.

And very early on, this trust was built in our relationships and felt as real as the Wonder Bread our sandwiches were made on. They were things you could count on.

Because trust runs deep within all of us.

Trust is the actual foundation of being willing to bite into Joey's apple after he's already eaten half. It's the willingness to share your lunch because why not? *Because there was no why not.* "Why not" would have meant:

I. Don't. Trust.

And yet those days are fading to black as the digital world grows. Sally is on Facebook now and has edited out some if not all of her freckles. *Bummer.* Billy had surgery to get rid of his birthmark. Why? It started with the bullying. But his parents didn't agree to to let him do the surgery until when?

Junior year in High School when Billy started wanting to date.

We didn't care when Billy was 9, but now he's 19 and well, Page365 is not enough. The birthmark has gotta go.

So what is happening here is that these changes have been occurring like an Amtrak train clickety-clacking along life's track and when a few freckles disappear or Joe's hair looks a tad colored you really don't pay too much attention. Sally's profile pic looks good. That's all we need to know. Life is Busy. We move on.

Then one day you run into Sally and *you* experience a *Facebreak.*

I have experienced this personally and I can tell you first hand it's a shocker. I don't care who you are. For that split second you think you're in a Salvador Dali Painting or a Fellini Movie. It's so fucking weird you lose grip for a *split second* with reality.

Reality has been slipping away since the day you had a friend offer you a bite of their apple and you said, "No, thanks."

You can cite all kinds of reasons why "that's not healthy to do that" or "You don't know what kind of germs the other person has," etc.

Nah. That's *crap.* Our good friend "Trust" has taken a hit for so long that when we *do* see a picture online we want to reach down into the last bit of our *trust reservoir* and *trust* that *Joe's pic is Joe.* We want to believe that that pic of *Sally is Sally.*

We want to believe.

And when our basic sense of trust or believability begins to shatter we, in fact, do not have a foundation. Think about that for a moment.

If you cannot trust what you see, then what do you have?

You have at that very instant the first seed of doubt. And doubt is you opening up Billy's cheese sandwich to see if you can trust that his Mom didn't put stale dated cheese on it. And when you go there, *you have left the world of trust, integrity, and love for your fellow man.* You have entered the world of cynicism and distrust and your own world will become tainted with this. You will begin to look at your "friends" with a bit more critical eye.

And when you've gone *that* far into that Murky Milky Way, I can tell you unequivocally *you have lost your way.* You open the door to skepticism and wiping off the top of the water bottle because now you can't trust just taking a swig. Your friend for a moment thinks to himself, *"Geezus Mike, it's fucking water. Not the bubonic plague."*

And as long as part of your life is lived online via your desktop, laptop, iPad, or smartphone, you will be interacting digitally. When you look at all the editing that's going on before you or I see the final picture or video, it begins to dawn on you we're all, to some degree or another, just producing and editing movies.

Jill: *"Ummm...I'm sorry...I recognize you from Facebook, but I um..forgot your name?"*

Martin: *"No probs. I'm Martin. Martin Scorsese."*

Megan: *"Honey, can you take another picture of me? Sorry, I know how frustrating this can be. I just looked fat in that picture. And I don't like that side of my face. It makes my nose look big."*

Freeze Frame.

Megan your nose *is* big. That's *your* nose. Your husband married you with it which means he loves you. Nose and all. *Show it to the world.*

And while we're at it, has anyone seen Sally? I want to see her at 52 with those freckles.

And hey Billy, if you're out there let me see that crooked front tooth of yours because you know Billy, that made you who you were man!

Okay campers, one last rant about fake and false. These *Facebreaks* are truly *not* the biggest break of them all.

Facebreaks are just the digital world shaking your hand and waking you up to the callouses on its real world hand.

The real break is the *break in reality* with what you are experiencing when you walk over to the cashier with your Facebook friend. You don't know how to act. You wing it. You will laugh at jokes that aren't funny. You will complement his humor. You will tell her you like her dress. Some of it sincere. Some of it out of the nervous anxiety of straddling these two worlds. And then the coffee date ends and you drive home you are not sure what really happened back there. You turn on your radio and some old tune from High School comes on and your mind wanders back to that time. And then the song ends and you turn off the radio and your mind goes back to you and Billy or Sally at recess when you were nine.

You remember that peanut butter and jelly sandwich. You recall Billy's laugh. His crooked front tooth. You remember that birthmark.

Man o' man.

You are consumed with that memory like it was yesterday. You think about it all the way home, because why?

Because that was real and what you just experienced was edited.

That's not just a *Facebreak*.

That's a reality break with real life.

And thousands upon thousands of people are experiencing this every hour of every day.

Facebreak: Final Chapter

To Click or Not to Click: Over to You

Alright, here we are at the final chapter of this excursion behind the curtain of Facebook. We've been down the Rabbit Hole and we saw the Red King and the Red Queen without their faces edited. The Rabbit himself was much older than his picture, but we had a good laugh because we chased the younger version and if you can't laugh at that than you need to go chase more rabbits.

We got introduced or possibly *reintroduced* to the Invisible line. Hopefully you know the coordinates for that line so that you don't go all Sulu into Warp Speed and create Facebreak: The Dark Side.

Along the way we learned that our lives are possibly more multidimensional than we were aware of. We might sit alone in a coffee shop after having met Sally with the freckles and realize she didn't just have them Photoshopped-out on Facebook when she turned 40, but she felt her freckles needed to be permanently removed so she made her appointment in Beverly hills and *whoosh*, they were gone.

Sally without freckles is...well...*different.*

Yet this is the world we live in now. And hopefully we're wiser now. This is how life *is*. If we're smart and we look at the glass as half full, we realize that Sally still laughs like Sally when we were eleven. It's a heartier laugh. It's got *depth* to it, and the missing freckles become insignificant because *thank god* nobody's figured out how to edit out that real life laugh.

And when you and Sally wrap up your coffee and conversation you hug---a *real* hug. Something that reminds you when you first got a hug from your Aunt or a girlfriend that really had *meaning* behind it. You realize in that moment that the realness of peanut butter and jelly sandwiches still exist. For a split second you understand that this is truly the best part of life: The connection to another soul. The human connection that all the Photoshopping in the world can not change.

And when you break from that hug there is an exchange between you and Sally and you each just know: *We made it.* We made it down and through the Rabbit Hole and came out the other side, *Facebreak* scars and all. And we're wiser for it. No words are exchanged. It's just a knowingness having both Walked when the Don't Walk Sign came on. We crossed the Invisible line without saying how or what or with whom. In that parting eye-to-eye contact there was this unspoken understanding of a shared history that we've both had our hearts broken. That we've both endured soul shattering experiences and yet *here we are.* A tad bit worn from the experience. Maybe a bit of surgery to just feel better about ourselves so that we can continue on.

Because hey, we've got a lot more livin' to do, right?

And for all the comments about Page365 and editing selfies and Photoshopping you walk away thinking that that is just part of life too. It's not bad or good or anything. It's just **How Life Is**. And possibly you look at the courage it took for Sally to do what she did and that all she was really looking for was what she was looking for on the playground when she was eleven: *A real friend. A connection.* She was so happy to have coffee you'd thought it was Christmas.

As you walk back to your car the thought comes to your mind that Sally *knew* you'd see her cosmetic changes, right? And right then your admiration for her goes out the roof way because that takes enormous courage to do that.

Well Sally changed her face, but not her personality. And I hope up the time track into the future I never have a coffee with a Sally that is an autobot. Maybe that will be my next book: *Facebot*: How Relationships Suffer from Dated Pentium Chips.

Crikey.

Sally: *"Sorry I'm late Dave. The circuitry in my right arm blew a fuse and I sat there laughing because I couldn't put the key in the ignition! LOL!*

Freeze Frame.

Okay, if we go all autobots in the future like something out of Blade Runner, do not, I repeat **do not** put in their AI (Artificial Intelligence) any of these acronyms: LOL, LMAO, ROFL. It is friggin' creepy enough having coffee with an autobot, but an autobot that's programmed to say LOL? That's just going over the edge. I swear I will raise the dead and send Gomer Pyle after you if you do that. I'm talking to you amped up Red Bull drinking software engineers out there.

Okay end of rant...back to reality...

So let's take a last look at this part that is underneath it all. The true underneath story of *you*, *you and your partner*, and what all of this means in relationship to *Life*.

I tried throughout this book to inject some humor into these situations because quite frankly there were real people with real *Facebreaks* that answered my original survey questions.

And the thing I admired most about these people is they had the courage to communicate some *very personal experiences* that had in fact affected if not fractured their own personal lives and especially their relationships.

In my profession I spend my days helping couples overcome these points of conflict and upset. See, Greg and Cindy *are you and your partner*. You are on this boat together and you see this *Facebreak torpedo* hurling through the water coming directly at you. You saw the "Like." You saw the "Heart." That torpedo is fueled with anger, jealousy, betrayal, sadness, shock. It's *loaded*.

But you're never really ready for what happens *on impact*. The mutual discovery of seeing the picture of the Greg and Cindy on the beach in Maui and your stomach sinking as low as it could go. The pictures your wife was looking at of her ex and how buff he is and you're not.

That's impact.

And although your relationship takes a hit, your attention is now riveted on *whether you will make it together*. Or will your relationship slowly take on water and you'll be forced to abandon ship and each swim away in new and different direction?

It's a great question to ask because both people experience the hit differently. When you experience something that rocks your relationship to its core and it's not the same for your mate, there *is* a separation occurring. The sound of fiberglass floorboards slowly cracking beneath you is uncomfortably present.

Your experience of the *Facebreak* is different than how *your partner* experienced it. Fractures in your soul are an interesting beast. They don't erase like they did on a blackboard in 6th grade.

And that incident will eventually fade and you get back on track and life is good again. Until Greg stumbles upon Cindy's history of looking at her exes football pics in her browser history. And that's something that you need to be acutely aware of. Although these somewhat minor infractions seem insignificant, they are in truth just the opposite because:

Facebreaks accumulate.

Facebreaks are in fact snapshots or pictures of a moment when the invisible line *was* crossed. Like a little kid out on the farm and not knowing any better you reach through the fence to pet the nice brown cow and your hand just slightly grazes that fence and you get *shocked.*

You will *never* forget that experience as long as you live because it wasn't just the physical shock. It wasn't. That went away after about fifteen minutes. But the rest of your day as a child your mind was trying to reconcile *what the hell?*

That's right. Enter our good friend Trust. As a kid you trusted that a fence was a fence. It's not so much anymore. Some fences are electric.

And not unlike *Facebreaks*, they shock your body, mind, *and* soul.

And so you experience these tiny little electric *Facebreak* shocks like a Taser shot to your heart. After suffering a *Facebreak* with your partner, your soul is like *what the hell?*

And even when you get past that and you run into another incoming Facebreak missile, you begin to feel like *maybe love doesn't work.* You withstand the hit and you "put on your big boy pants" and *take a deep breath.* You look out the window and think maybe the fairy tale idea of holding hands together on the beach when you are eighty years old is just that: A Fairy Tale.

The truth is the Fairy Tale is very much alive. As cornball as that sounds, *it is.* Just because you found out your Prince Charming actually dyed his hair or there was a reason your Cinderella needed that corset tied by all those birds and mice, it doesn't take away from the dream you had. It doesn't. Any story, whether yours or from a book or movie, always have antagonists. There's always a dark side or a chasm or something that challenges the good. *Always.*

Facebook provides enormous good and value for people and their families all over the world. But there is a chasm. A rabbit hole. A hidden revolving bookcase if you will. And that's the province of the Invisible Line vs. your own Personal Integrity.

The foundation for you and your partner *is built on integrity.* That's why it's so violent when there's a transgression. Confession has in its roots the very fact that you *need* to confess. You need to finally say it when your Mom asks you if it was you who took the cookies out of the cookie jar and you see the chocolate chip smudges on your hand:

"Yep, I did. I took the cookies out of the cookie jar."

And right then time stops. You are looking up at your Mom and you're sure she's going to *go all Godzilla on you* and breathe fire on your ass until you're just a lump of charcoal.

But something else happens this time.

This time *truth* got to her before she morphed into Godzilla.

When the truth hit your Mom for a split second *she's not sure she heard it.* She's so use to lies and shit bringing up two boys and a girl she was just *shocked.* But Mom knew this friend of ours. She *knew truth* when she heard it. And then you see something as a kid you hardly ever saw: A single tear starts to roll down your Mom's face as she reaches down to hug you. It's all still in slow motion but there's that *real hug.* And damn. You think to yourself:

It's okay to tell the truth.

And that's all you need to do with your partner. And believe me this is one of *the* most difficult things for partners to do with each other. It sounds easy. It's not. If it were we'd all be doing it like sipping an iced tea. The reason it's not easy is this:

When tell the truth you fear that this will hurt your partner worse than the lie. I know, right? It's *crazy*. But that's the truth. So you buffer it. You put a curve in it. You alter it just slightly so it doesn't hit them so hard.

But here's the thing most everyone overlooks. We've all lied and been lied to for *sooooo lonnnngg* that we are at many instances at *our breaking point.* See it's why your partner or you can get so livid about a "Like." It's <u>not</u> the Like. It's the fact that it was *hidden.* It was not out there in the open where truth resided. You know all this "transparency" shit people talk about today? That's just marketers giving a new name to *truth.* How much more transparent can you get than the truth? Friggin' marketing bullshit. Wow, okay that was *"a mini-rant"* right there.

So look by not letting truth breathe you just suffocated your partner a tad and you moved that needle closer to the breaking point. So you're getting the emotional blowback of a lifetime of not just being straight. That's why it's a *Facebreak.*

It's like dropping fine China. It *will* break. And despite some great superglue repair, forever after that China is *just not the same.* Breaks do that to a being.

Mistakes lead to Facebreaks lead to Heartbreaks.

So as you go forward you understand that in your relationship and life there going to be rough waters. There are going to be shouting matches and torpedoes and things said and done that make you sometimes *wonder why you ever got on that boat together.*

And then when the weather is calm and your boyfriend or husband sends you some flowers or writes a rare love note to you, *you feel that it's all been worth it.* Or when your girlfriend or wife sets the table with some candles and Bocelli is playing in the background and she *did* make that *amazing* spaghetti sauce that *this woman is the greatest love of your life.*

It is those moments of reflection where *you,* the being or spirit, review your life with all the scars and fractures as a whole. And having won against *all of that* somewhere deep inside your soul you have a moment of clarity: Those Facebook torpedoes and ridiculous escapades down the Facebook Rabbit Hole *were in fact not something that broke you.*

They were in fact things that defined you.

The *Facebreaks,* although disruptive and seemingly soul destroying, in the end *did not divide you or your partner.*

And you learned either by falling down that Rabbit Hole and skinning your knees or being hood-winked by some photoshopped picture, *that it was your adventure created by you all along.*

It was *you* who decided to follow the Rabbit. *You* decided to go down the Rabbit Hole. It was *your* finger that hit the Enter key when you *liked and shared and hearted.*

You. Did. It. All.

And because you know it was *you* who decided to Walk, when the Don't Walk Sign was flashing *you own it* and *take responsibility for it.*

And if you do that and become better buddies with the truth, you are going to be okay. You will make it the rest of the way.

And when you realize that *you* have the power of choice *to click or not to click* and send your life's adventure or story in an entirely different direction, then by that very power you become more observant and more respectful of your partner.

*Because even though you're sitting in your office alone or in the other room in your house, it's not just **you** in that boat.*

And maybe you begin to see that your keystrokes are not something that just define you, but they have the power to affect another person's feelings and thoughts and Life. That "simple innocuous Like" can be the difference between making love or sleeping in separate rooms.

It might be hard to imagine that your decisions or keystrokes could have *that* much power. But in truth they do. All of the survey answers that became this book started with the Invisible Line and then a finger or fingers typing away on a keyboard.

"Lions, and Tigers and Bears! Oh My!"

"Fingers and Keyboards and Likes! Oh My!"

And because you do have enormous power, *responsibility* for using that power does come into play. You could light that match as a kid with wonder and curiosity. But when that fire gulped some oxygen and that lone piece of paper caught fire to the rest of your trashcan and your Mom came charging in yelling expletives you never heard come out of her mouth, well you learned that *your* little fingers and that little match had more power than you thought.

You and Your Partner:

When I get together to help couples usually there is an Invisible Line Moment (ILM).

Freeze frame.

Geezus. See? I've got the acronym virus in me. I gotta get it out. I'm having an *Acrobreak.* Damn...that's a good one right there...

Okay so when I enter the picture the ILM has gone all afterburner and both people are jettisoning more shit than NASA can deal with.

And this is from a *Facebreak!* Actually it's never just *one.* I told you they *accumulate.* Jeff says Susan did *this.* Susan says Jeff did *that.* Jeff brings up a *zinger* about Susan he was saving. Probably *Save As.* And Susan is all like *yougottabefuckingkiddingme* so she reaches into her Kryptonite file and brings up the BIG REVEAL about Jeff & Amanda.

Swear to god it's a good thing you cannot buy flamethrowers because these two would pull out the big guns. And Detective Dave sits them down and we go back before they did all this clickin' n' and hidin' and shit and what do we find?

Jeff and Susan were doing just fine.

It's. Fucking. Amazing.

Remember the kid with the match?

Here's the thing: All you hear about with relationship problems is the trashcan on fire and Mom all bug-eyed swearing like a sailor.

Looks bad when you see *the end of that scenario.*

But before that match was ever lit, little Billy was bored and had some free time on his hands. He saw that box of matches and well, he got an invitation from Temptation and the rest is history.

When we go back before Jeff and Susan's *Facebreak,* sure enough they were just playing with matches. *"Wow, my ex just got engaged...holy crap she's young...let me go check out...*

See?

That's a fire right there.

The Wild Wild West.

So listen. You're going to play with matches as long as you're human and breathe and have wonder in your soul. Let's not get all "Don't Play with Matches," and shit. That kind of admonition is *why* you played with them.

The better idea is to get a better understanding of *what it is that is challenging your personal values and integrity.*

See it's *not* out there in the picture of Jennifer and her low-cut top staring at you from her Facebook Profile Picture. It's *not.*

It's not your ex grinning like he's grinning right at you because he's got a much younger *and-oh-by-the-way* beautiful new girlfriend.

It's *not* that. Yes, I know when you see these pics you get some emotion swelling up in you whether you are the guy looking at Brittany's boobs or the gal looking at her ex. I mean there it is sitting in front of you with all that HD color and iPhone pixelated brilliance.

But if you bite on that, then you need more Jedi training. Remember "There is no try, there is only Do?" Well little Yoda left out:

"There is only Look, not Click."

I know. Looking in the Wild Wild West is like just looking at the saloon girls and that's it. What fun is that?

What fun was it really clickin? *Maybe for that moment.* But no saloon girl or Mr. Rich Guy with the Lamborghini ever set your soul on fire or made your heart skip a beat.

When you met your partner and they met you your heart *did* skip a beat. Your soul *was* on fire. Those were the only matches you needed. And you think because your relationship has lost some of that fire you'll play with some new matches.

That's the oldest trick in the book. That's pre-Wild Wild West.

Beings have been hoodwinked and seduced and tempted since the beginning of time. It's part of our glorious spiritual Achilles heel.

Somewhere, sometime, you gotta get smarter. You gotta be like James Garner in the Rockford files. Or Columbo. Or Gibbs, that CSI guy. You gotta get smarter, *right?*

Because chicks will keep struttin' their stuff online and guys abs and bods will always look better. Always. That's the revolving bookcase.

So save yourself some future *Facebreaks* and *Look, Don't Click.* Or if that's too preachy or too Yoda...

Look, Click, and Share with your Partner.

Let your friend the *Truth* breathe out there in the daylight.

After all, those chocolate chip smudges on your hand are just reminding you that you can't really hide shit, right?

And remember your partner may or may not be as forgiving as Billy's Mom in that slow-motion moment.

He or she in real time may indeed *go all Godzilla on you.*

If they do...*give me a call.*

Note: The purpose of this book is to provide some insight and raise people's awareness to real situations that are occurring in relationships and marriages all across the world. If you know someone that would benefit from reading this book, please take a moment and go to Amazon.com and leave a review. Thank you.

Biography:

Dave Worthen is an International Speaker, Consultant, Counselor, and Coach.

He has a private practice in Clearwater, Florida and has been coaching professionals and their families for over forty years.

As part of his passion to help other people, Dave has traveled as far away as Russia, Ukraine, France, Norway, and Sweden to give seminars and workshops to help individuals and couples in their marriages and relationships.

He is currently working on his next book as a follow-up to Facebreak giving a behind the scenes look at the effects of Facebreaks in the workplace.

When Dave is not working with couples you'll find him running on the beach before the sunrises early in the morning.

His favorite activities are writing, reading, photography, and giving seminars to help people improve their lives.

He can be contacted for a free private consultation at daveworthen.com or by email at daveworthen@gmail.com

52967547R00079

Made in the USA
San Bernardino, CA
04 September 2017